T0346456

'My meeting with Feby Herewila [...] Kerobokan Prison has left a deep [...] heart. God can change a broken ves. [...] or a future, into a priceless, pure gold one. Feby has helped Andrew and many other people find the straight path that leads to the true eternity.

'Death is not a tragic event and death is not an end. But how we walk on this earth is what matters. Even though we are bound in a physical body, God's power cannot be contained by anything at all. His power is above all things. His power brings light into darkness.

'*Walking Him Home* brings motivation and enlightenment as to how we can live a life for God and others – a life that leads people to the true path of eternal salvation.'

Dr Daniel H Pandji,
National Coordinator of My Home Indonesia

'This story was prepared by God. God prepared Feby for something much bigger than herself so that the will of God could be realised. There are many things God will do in Feby's life. The fact that Feby is still here with this book shows that, in all walks of life, through God, there is always room for a new sense of hope and joy to welcome him in our lives.'

Jonathan Pattiasina, pastor,
Founder of Garam Ministry Melbourne

'*Walking Him Home* is such an inspiring story of faith. The beautiful thing is how that faith stays true through not only the joyful moments of life but also as she walks through the valley of the shadow of death. This account of how she met Andrew Chan and how together they worshipped in the midst of tremendous challenge is one I'll never forget. Since first hearing their story, I have often thought about this – that if it is possible to worship Jesus while facing down the barrel of a gun, then it's surely possible to face anything in this life and still be found with a song of praise, hope and trust on our lips, and in our hearts. This book will stir up your faith in the Living God.'

Matt Redman, worship leader and songwriter

'Feby Herewila's vivid account of her life growing up in Indonesia, her walk with Jesus, marriage to Australian prisoner-turned-pastor Andrew Chan and dedication to an awe-inspiring ministry, is a life-changing experience. Feby's journey is so deeply connected to a profound sense of purpose, faith and love that it will encourage men and women, young and old, to seek the heart of God, find breakthrough and live a truly significant life of humility, joy and servanthood.'

Marc Furmie, film-maker, screenwriter

'Perhaps you've questioned God when prayers have not been answered. Perhaps your faith and trust have been shaken. Then this book is for you. It will provoke you and challenge your certainties. It will answer many of the questions that may have troubled you for years and it will draw you into a closer walk with God the Father, God the Son and with the Holy Spirit. I recommend it without reservation.'

Dr Ernest Frank Crocker, author, speaker, physician and photographer

Walking Him Home

Learning to hope again after loving and losing Andrew Chan on death row

Feby Chan with Naomi Reed

Authentic

First published 2021 by Authentic Media Limited,
PO Box 6326, Bletchley, Milton Keynes, MK1 9GG.
authenticmedia.co.uk

British Library Cataloguing in Publication Data
A catalogue record for this book is available from the British Library.
ISBN: 978-1-78893-216-5
978-1-78893-217-2 (e-book)

Cover design by Dimentrus
Printed and bound in Great Britain by Bell & Bain Ltd, Glasgow

With gratefulness, I dedicate this book to Jesus Christ, the love and the author of my life, and to Andrew Chan, who brought so much joy to me.

Contents

1

It Started with God

*As the heavens are higher than the earth, so are
my ways higher than your ways and my thoughts
than your thoughts.*

Isaiah 55:9

People often ask me, 'Why did you marry someone on death row? Why did you visit Kerobokan Prison in the first place? Why did you start dating someone who had been sentenced to death for drug trafficking?'

They wonder all sorts of things. Perhaps they think that it was 'bad boy' syndrome. Was I drawn to a 'bad boy' in need of transformation? Was Andrew a bad boy? Or, was I someone who needed to be needed? Did I have the kind of personality that couldn't exist without helping someone in dire circumstances? Or, perhaps, I was young and naïve, and carried away by blind love, not considering any of the ramifications?

I tell them that it started with God. It wasn't my idea at all.

I was born into a Christian family, in 1980, in Kupang. Kupang is the largest city and the capital of West Timor, which is 2,000 kilometres east of Java, the main island of Indonesia. Indonesia is actually made up of more than 17,000 islands, and West Timor is in the eastern area. Indonesia also has the largest Muslim population in the world, although we are not an Islamic state. We are a democratic republic. In West Timor, though, the majority of the population are Christian. Kupang itself is a port city. It is significantly hotter and dryer than the rest of Indonesia. Java's rainy season, for example, goes all the way from December to May, but in Kupang it only rains until February. As well as that, Kupang tends to be multiethnic and the people are friendly and warm towards each other. When they walk, they hold hands. When they talk, they're very straightforward. Timorese people always greet each other with a nose-to-nose kiss. They would never do that in Java!

Back when I was born, my father was working with the government administration in Kupang, so we were provided with a house on the compound near the governor's office. My father came from a Christian family but my mother's background was Muslim. Her family used to fast three times a week, as Javanese Muslims. They were apparently quite strict, not eating meat or vegetables on those days. But, even back then, my mother said that she had experiences of God while she prayed and fasted. She had questions and she wanted to know more of God. Then she met my father.

In those days, my mother's family were also living quite close to the governor's house, so that's how my parents met. Not long afterwards, my mother asked my father some of her questions about God. My father shared the gospel with her. He said that Jesus is God's Son and that Jesus is the only way we can know God.

It was unusual, of course, for someone from a Christian family to date someone from a Muslim family, but my mother's parents weren't radical Muslims, and they mostly just kept telling my mother to be careful. They said, 'Don't do anything that ruins the family name.'

Not long after that, my parents were married in Kupang, and they started going to a local Christian church. During that time, my mother started to understand the gospel. She believed in Jesus and she became very faithful in her new beliefs. She always went to church. There were times when my father didn't wake up in time to go to church, but my mother always went. She wanted to go.

My parents had eleven children in that house in Kupang, near the governor's house, and I was their tenth child. Nine of us were girls. It's the same area of Kupang that is now known as the old city. Our house was a single-storey brick house, with about ten bedrooms. But the bedrooms were added, bit by bit, by my father, as we grew in number. He began by building the back part himself, then he slowly added bedrooms and then he finished the front part of the house, creating a little garden by the entrance.

In those days, both of my parents loved to play tennis. They were involved in many tournaments in Kupang and they won quite a few of them. But my mother didn't want me to play tennis. She said that I had scoliosis – curvature of the spine – and that playing tennis might make it worse. So instead, we all played table tennis and volleyball. We had a table tennis table set up in the back area and all the neighbourhood kids would come to play with us. I remember one year, when I was in kindergarten, my father bought us all roller skates. My elder siblings were allowed to skate up and down the street, but I wasn't allowed out. So I skated all around the house and I thought it was great.

The thing that I remember most about my childhood, though, is the prayer meetings. Every Tuesday afternoon, my parents would hold a prayer meeting in our house, and a great crowd would come from all over the neighbourhood and from further away as well. Everyone was welcome to come to worship God and pray together. They would start arriving at our house at about 4 p.m. and it would go on until about 7 p.m. Our living room was always full of people, praying and singing and worshipping God. It was a large space – about 7 metres by 12 metres – and the people would crowd in, sitting on the floor, on the carpet, praying earnestly for hours and hours.

It had an amazing influence on me. From that time, when I was about 12, I also began to pray, and I always expected God to speak. I would wake up in the morning and read my Bible and pray before I went to school. Of course, back then, I was praying mostly for my studies and for other people at my school. I remember that I was begging and pleading with God so earnestly. I wanted my studies to go well so that I could be first in the class! Also, back then, there was someone in my class who annoyed me, so I prayed for her. After a while, that person stopped annoying me! I kept praying earnestly and I saw more answers to prayer. Nobody taught me how to pray; I just prayed. But I don't think I fully understood who God was. I certainly didn't realise that his plans aren't always our plans, and that his ways aren't always our ways.

My mother used to regularly share with me about her own experiences of prayer. She said that, years earlier, a friend of theirs had had a bad accident. He was in a coma in a hospital in Kupang. But at the time my parents were staying in Yogyakarta, Java, visiting my mother's parents. It was in the 1980s, so there were no telephones or other means of communication, and my parents couldn't do anything. They couldn't visit their friend because they couldn't get a flight from where they were in Yogyakarta back to Kupang . . . but they wanted to be there! So, instead, my parents knelt down, and they prayed together earnestly, in agreement. They prayed and prayed for the worker. They so wanted to see him before he died. Then the next day, they were, amazingly, able to send a telegram and book a flight from Yogyakarta to Kupang. They went straight to the hospital and they saw their friend. They were able to sit down with him and talk to him, and then minutes later, their friend died.

Because of that, my mother told me over and over again that there is power in prayer. She said that when two people agree and pray together, especially a husband and wife, there is power. She would always read to us from Matthew 18:19,20:

> [Jesus said,] 'Truly I tell you that if two of you on earth agree about anything they ask for, it will be done for them by my Father in heaven. For where two or three gather in my name, there am I with them.'

God hears us, she said, and God is powerful and able. He is at work in the world and in our lives, for his glory. My mother always told me to pray, ever since I was a little child. She herself was so prayerful that everyone from the town used to come to her and ask her what to do because they knew that she prayed to God. She was simple, but she was very strong, mentally. If she heard from God, she would be so sure. You could never argue with her. She would tell everybody what she had heard from God, and she was so confident. We loved her. We loved her character and her dress sense and etiquette. She was raised very properly, and she was always telling us about correct behaviour and how to show respect to others. But mostly she prayed, and I grew up seeing the effects of her prayer life. I copied her. All my siblings were the same. My younger sister always had dreams – that's how God spoke to her – and my older sister had the gift of interpreting her dreams. Then another sister received the gift of words from God (see 1 Cor. 14:6). Every time we prayed, God gave her a verse, and direction through his Word in the Bible.

I spent my teenage years like that, praying every morning in a disciplined way. I saw so many answers to prayer . . . but I don't think I had a very deep relationship with God. I was reading the Bible like a textbook.

Then something very difficult happened. My father died in 1995, when I was in high school. I was only 15. He died from kidney failure. He was only ill for a week. The head of the whole region came to visit our house when he heard that my dad was sick. And when he saw how ill my dad was, he said to him, 'Don't rely on the medical system here in Kupang. It's not good enough. You need to go to Java.'

So then my mum and my dad and my eldest brother flew from Kupang to Java to get better treatment. My dad stayed in a hospital in Surabaya, in East Java, for three days – and that's where he died, in Java, far away from us.

I was so close to my dad. He was like a big, shady tree for the whole family. He would pick me up from school and read my reports with me and help me with my school work. He was the one who taught me English and maths. He helped me with my essays all the way through high school. He used to cut my hair. He even cut it like Princess Diana's hair one year. He would see something on the television and he would try that new hairstyle on me.

The news of his death hit us really badly as a family. I remember that my auntie came to tell us while the rest of us were waiting in the house. I couldn't believe it. I ran out of the house, barefoot, all the way up and down the street, crying and crying. Even the neighbours came out and they said, 'Are you sure that he's dead?'

It happened so very quickly – within one week. None of us could believe it. Two days later, they brought his body back to our house. I could hear the ambulance and the police escort coming from afar. But I was still in denial. I was hoping it wasn't real. As the noise came closer, I closed my eyes. I didn't want to see it. Then they took my dad's body and laid it on a bed in the centre of our living room, so that everyone could come and pay their respects to him.

I refused to go near his body. I waited until the next day. Then my brother said to me, 'Feby, you have to go and see the body.' He took me to the edge of the bed and he said, 'Try to look at the end of the bed first [his feet], then let your eyes travel further up, until you see his face. It will be easier then.'

I did what my brother said. I slowly looked at the end of the bed and then at the body of my dad. Then I felt his hand in my hand. He was so cold! He had always been so warm. I couldn't believe it. I was in shock.

The funeral was held three days later. I cried and cried. First, they took my dad's body to the government office so that all his colleagues could pay their respects. Then they took him to the cemetery. We were following along behind. At one point, I looked behind me, and there were so many cars and people! They were filling the streets for as far as I could see. My dad was so well loved and respected.

My mum told me that before that, even if my father went away for a few days for work, she missed him. How would she cope now, without him? There were eleven of us and the burden was immediately on her. Everybody had adored my dad.

He had been taking care of so many people in the extended family and we had all felt special to him. So when he died, everyone lost something to hold on to. We grieved terribly.

Before my dad died, I remember, he would come home for lunch or dinner. In Indonesian culture, you are meant to separate the food onto two plates – one plate is for the parents and the other plate is for the children. The parents normally eat their plate first and they keep it separate. But my dad would always leave some of his food for me. My mum would say, 'He really loves you!' If he ever went to a function, he would bring back something special for me, like a piece of cake or a sweet. But we all felt like that. I don't know how he did it. He treated each of us as if we were special, and we enjoyed that feeling. We also enjoyed his protection. My dad was one of the leaders of the political parties in government in Timor at the time, so there was a lot of respect for him. Even when he collected us from school, we would all walk taller as we walked out of the school gate with him.

So after he died, it was very, very hard. We didn't know how to be us any more. My mum kept working. She had food stalls. She would bake bread every morning and throughout the day, and sell it at the stalls. At the end of the first school year after my dad died, I remember that I forgot to tell someone to collect my school report. Normally my dad did it. But, eventually, my brother stepped in and he took care of me. He was eleven years older than me, so he collected my school reports and he drove me to birthday parties.

There's a saying in Indonesia that if your mum dies, you lose the love in your house, but if your dad dies, you lose the respect in your house. For people in Indonesia, the respect comes from the father, especially for girls. And there were nine of us girls in our family. I remember the first time our whole family went out for dinner after my dad died. We were sitting in the restaurant, and we saw one of my father's friends at another table. He had been such a good friend of my father. And then he saw us – but he just ignored us. My mum was shocked. Normally, he would have come and said hello. My mum was about to get up and go to speak to him, but my brother told her to sit down. He said that the friend had definitely seen us and that he obviously no longer wanted to speak to us. Our situation had changed. It happened like that a few more times, and we began to realise that, as a family, we were no longer worthy of a conversation. We were bereft. Our father had gone and we felt his absence every day. My sisters cried every night. I just wanted him to be there.

After a while, I started to pray about it. I didn't know who to hold on to. But I realised that my only choice was to hold on to God. I think the main thing that changed for all of us as a family was that we started to see God as our Father. It happened slowly, over time, but we all said that it brought us closer to God, especially my older sisters. We didn't have a choice. He was our Father.

In 1998, I finished school in Kupang, and the following year I moved to Yogyakarta, Central Java, to study graphic design. My sisters were already there, studying. I had actually wanted to be an architect, but my elder brother was already an architect, and he told me that he didn't think I would be able to do it. He said, 'You have to work very hard, always drawing and doing assignments. I don't think you can handle that because you are not very strong. Choose something else!'

So I did what my brother advised. I took a one-year break and moved to Yogyakarta in 1999. I stayed there with my two sisters, who were a few years older than me. They were already involved in the church there. After a while, I realised that my

brother was perhaps right. I did have back pain from my scoliosis and I often had headaches. I was not very strong. Then,
one day, my sisters said to me, 'Did you know that Jesus can
heal your back pain?'

I knew that God could do anything, but I hadn't really
thought about him healing my back pain or my headaches.
At the same time, my sisters told me about personal salvation
through Jesus. They said that I had to make a choice to receive
Jesus. Up until then, I had always thought that religion was an
inheritance. I was a Christian because my mum and dad were
Christians. Everybody in Indonesia thought like that. But that
day, my sisters told me that I could receive Jesus as my personal
Saviour. So I prayed for that. I really wanted to know Jesus
more and more. I also said to them, 'If my back will be healed,
then I will be baptised.'

I really wanted to be healed – and that week I was actually
healed. It was amazing. I received Jesus as my personal Saviour,
and I was baptised in a local pool. As they prayed for my
back, it was completely healed in that moment. Before that,
I couldn't even sit for one hour without being in a lot of pain.
Throughout my teenage years I'd had constant headaches,
especially when I was travelling in the car or on a motorbike.
But that week I received Jesus as my Saviour, I was baptised and
I was completely healed! I didn't have back pain or headaches
ever again after that.

That was the beginning of my walk with Jesus – the beginning of my radical story of following him. I had no idea, of
course, what it would mean or what was coming next.

2

The Presence of God

*How much more will your Father in heaven give
the Holy Spirit to those who ask him!*

Luke 11:13

In the year 2000, as well as studying graphic design, I started to become more involved in the church in Yogyakarta, the church that my sisters attended. The more time I spent there, and the more I prayed, the more I really enjoyed being in the presence of God. In those days, our church had regular prayer meetings every Friday night and we saw so many miracles. Lots of people in the town and nearby community attended the meetings and many of them were healed and came to the Lord.

One time, I myself became very sick. It was a strange and sudden allergy. I had swelling all over my body and I was vomiting. It went on like that for weeks. If I had clothes with elastic around my waist or my wrists, the whole area would become hot and red and swollen. I went to see a doctor about it and the doctor was very worried. He said that nothing could be done. He didn't know what it was. I asked the doctor why it had suddenly happened, and nobody knew what it was. Even my mother was shocked. Everything they tried made it worse.

So my mum took me back home to Kupang. She thought that, if I died, she would be able to bury me close to my dad, near the house in Kupang. But when I was back home, I started to pray. I knew that I was ill, so I prayed for three days for God to reveal to me what was wrong or what had gone wrong in my life. Was there something I could do? I remember that I was sitting on our front porch and praying, and as I did, I saw a picture in my mind of a childhood memory.

As a child, I had liked to hold my dad from behind. He would be wearing a singlet and I would climb onto his back, and he would lift me up and give me a piggyback. But he would also often scratch his back, and whenever he scratched his back, there was swelling. The picture of his swelling came into my mind as I prayed, and I wondered how the memory had come back to me. I was only little when that happened. But I knew that God had shown me something, so I went into my room and I prayed. I prayed that if it was a generational curse, that God would cut it off and break it in my life. In that moment, all the swelling and the allergy left me. I was well again!

That's when I started to see that beliefs from the past (especially pagan, dark beliefs) can be passed down from one generation to another, particularly in cultures like Indonesia where black magic is so common. Before that, I hadn't fully realised how strong it was. Growing up as Christians in Kupang, we hadn't heard that much about black magic because my parents hardly ever talked about it. But it was real . . . and that experience showed me profoundly about the power of prayer, pointing to a God who is powerful and present with us and who listens and cares.

Being well again, I returned to Yogyakarta, and I continued studying for my Diploma in Graphic Design. At the same time, I began to study various short Bible college courses in

Yogyakarta, and then, after a while, I was ordained as a pastor and employed by the church full-time, as an intercessor.

In Indonesia, it is very common for churches to employ people as intercessors and to have a prayer tower. The intercessors run the prayer meetings and they run the prayer tower. The prayer tower is a public space that is open twenty-four hours a day, for anyone who wants to come and pray. In a lot of churches, the prayer tower is in the highest place at the church, but our prayer tower was actually underground in the car park area. From inside our prayer room, we could see into the car park through two large windows. That was helpful because we could always see who was coming in or going out.

There were four of us employed as intercessors in the prayer tower back then, and we each had a six-hour time slot every day, taking it in turns to lead the prayer out loud for those six hours. We did it six days a week. Every two hours we had a break for fifteen minutes. That's also when I learned to play the guitar. I wanted to play worship songs to God, so I just started. It was so beautiful. When you spend that much time in the presence of God, your senses are very sharp. I often wish I could go back to that now!

Most of the time, though, I would be responsible for the time slot between midnight and 6 a.m. I really enjoyed it, although I did find the first two hours between midnight and 2 a.m. difficult. It can feel heavier than at other times of the day or night, partly because you're so sleepy, but also because of spiritual matters. Between midnight and 2 a.m., I would always see more visions – of black magic, and of people worshipping idols. You can feel it and see it. I think that God used that time to open my eyes to the different dimensions, especially while I was praying for the city, and to understand the heaviness of idol worship in Indonesia. There are so many strongholds capturing people's minds – especially in Yogyakarta, with thousands of students arriving each year, many of them practising black magic and bringing their customs and mantras with them. Can you imagine the mix? That's why we really needed to stand in prayer, to ask the Lord to guard the town.

But interestingly, once the clock hit 2.30 a.m., the atmosphere would suddenly change. We could see it and feel it. Maybe that's when the black magic stopped. It's hard to say. Maybe God took action. All this doesn't mean that God wasn't active, or stronger, or more powerful than the dark powers earlier in the evening, or all through the night. Of course he was, but he also allowed us to see what was going on in that other realm. Interestingly, those early hours in the morning were also when crime rates would tend to go up as well.

Mostly, those years of prayer showed me that God was sovereignly in charge and he longed for us to pray and to wait on him, within the reality of the spiritual realm – and that's what I did every morning, until 6 a.m. Then another person would come and take over. I would sleep for a few hours, then I would wake up and eat and continue with my other ministries in the church, usually involving the youth.

However, back in the prayer tower, there was always someone praying – and we weren't there to pray for our own personal matters. Our prayers were always focused on others: our city and the world. Of course, as we prayed, God spoke to us and we wrote everything down in a book. That was our other responsibility. Then, at the end of the month, we summarised the notes in the prayer book (and everything that God was trying to tell us about our church and our city). Our pastor would then pass the summary on to the whole church, so that we were all of one accord and so that we understood the movement of God.

It was an amazing time. I stayed in that role for five years, praying six hours a day, six days a week, from 2003 until the end of 2007. When I look back on that time now, I realise that it was when God really taught me how to pray and intercede, and how to wait on him. The Lord softened me. He showed me about his love, his grace and his mercy towards us, through Jesus. I became acutely aware of his voice and his leading, in everything. Looking back, I think it prepared me well for what was ahead, although I didn't know that back then.

In early 2007, I was praying about what I should do next. I had always wanted to study overseas at a Bible college, but I was worried about the expense. Years earlier, when my father had been alive, he had known of my longing to study abroad and he had said not to worry about the expense. He said that they – my parents – would find a way to help me. But then my father passed away, and when the time came for me to study, I worried. I remember one time I was praying about it. My friend had sent me seven brochures of different Bible colleges in other countries. They were all so expensive! How could I pay for them? I started to pray. I asked God to show me his will. I told him that I trusted that, if it was his will, he would make a way for me to study. Suddenly, as I was praying, I could hear the door behind me open. I heard someone walk into the room. The person stood right beside me and then said, 'Choose the best school. If your earthly father knows how to give good gifts to you, how much more does your heavenly Father care for you?'

Then the person left again through the door behind me and I sat there and cried. I felt so loved. I knew for sure that the Father's love for me was so very great! It was even greater than the love of my earthly father. Later, I read Luke 11:11–13:

> Which of you fathers, if your son asks for a fish, will give him a snake instead? Or if he asks for an egg, will give him a scorpion? If you then, though you are evil, know how to give good gifts to your children, how much more will your Father in heaven give the Holy Spirit to those who ask him!

After that, at the end of 2007, I moved to Singapore to study at a Bible college there. It was amazing how my heavenly Father provided for me! While I was in Singapore, I also took on a role in a local church, and I stayed there until 2010. I was on the pastoral staff, ministering to the Indonesian people attending that church in Singapore. It was a big church and I learned so much there. There were more than 3,000 people in the church, and the organisation was very professional and well-run. I realised that we often pray for a miracle, for revival in Indonesia, or for 3,000 people to hear about the Lord Jesus and to come to church. But you also need a structure to care for that many people. You can't just pray for them to come. That church in Singapore had such a good system in place to care for 3,000 people.

I also made many good friends there from other parts of the world, and I started to see the work of God beyond Indonesia. It showed me again that God's ways are so far beyond our imaginings. He is truly our loving heavenly Father, and we can't even begin to understand his ways or fathom his love for us and the world. We also can never predict what he wants to do next, in our lives or in the world.

3

A Strong Wind and a Big Fish

He has sent me to bind up the broken-hearted,
to proclaim freedom for the captives and release
from darkness for the prisoners . . .

Isaiah 61:1

In late 2010, I left Singapore and I returned to Yogyakarta, in Java. I was once again busy working full-time in the church as a pastor, and in the wider prayer ministry as an intercessor. I enjoyed being back with my friends at church, especially my closest friend and prayer partner, Linda, who I had met ten years earlier at a Friday evening prayer meeting in Yogyakarta.

I remember the night Linda first came to the prayer meeting. She was with her new husband and she seemed friendly straight away. We introduced ourselves and quickly became friends. We started to meet a few times a week to pray. On Saturday mornings, she would pick me up in her car, at about 4 a.m. She drove a large, bronze Suzuki minivan, and I would feel the anticipation as soon as I got in. We would quickly chat about where we wanted to go, and then I would pull out my guitar and we would drive all around Yogyakarta, both of us interceding for the city and singing and worshipping God. We always had a guitar!

It was so dark and quiet at 4 a.m., but that was the whole idea. It was the best time to pray. Nobody could see us and we could drive around the whole city of Yogyakarta and pray over it, especially for the young people. We would stop occasionally and pray over different areas, as the Spirit led us. Yogyakarta itself is a fairly large city. It has a population of well over four hundred thousand people and it has more than a hundred universities or smaller colleges. That's why there are so many young people on the streets. They even call it the 'student city', because people from all over Indonesia come there to study. On every corner in Yogyakarta, there's another university, and there are students everywhere, on motorbikes and in cars. Even really early in the morning, you can see students coming back from studying with their friends, or heading off to college. It's not a particularly fashionable city (not like Jakarta), although it is well-known for its batiks, art, puppetry, murals and dance, but mostly people go there to study. That's what they care about.

Yogyakarta is an ordered city. It has one large volcano to the north, known as Mount Merapi, and then Parangtritis Beach to the south. To the east, there is the famous Hindu temple, known as Prambanan, and then to the west, there is Borobudur – a Buddhist temple and a World Heritage site. In the middle of those four landmarks, there is the royal palace, right in the centre of the city. The palace has to be located on a single, direct line from Mount Merapi to the beach at the Indian Ocean. In Indonesia, the royalty, especially the king, have a practice of worshipping the Queen of the Southern Sea. She's a goddess from Javanese mythology, known as *Nyai Roro Kidul* and most people in Yogyakarta (apart from the Christians) believe in her. The kings, in particular, have to pay respect to the goddess, otherwise she may become angry and a tsunami will come. In most people's thinking, the goddess is very powerful, even today, and she always needs to be placated. People in Indonesia are generally very involved in black magic. They're always talking about the magic that they're using, for protection against curses or from poisoning or from people trying to harm them.

So there I would be with Linda, praying in her car and driving around the city at 4 a.m. We loved it! It would take us about fifteen minutes to fully wake up and start to concentrate in prayer. People say that if you spend fifteen minutes in prayer, you're really only beginning. You're just 'scratching the devil's back'. That's possibly true. But after fifteen minutes, I would be feeling refreshed and more awake. I would be concentrating in prayer and I would be in the right flow of worship. I would look forward to that! Also, when you pray a lot for other people rather than for yourself, everything is different. As we prayed, we would often get a verse or a vision or a word from God about something or someone to pray for in Yogyakarta or Indonesia. And then, later in the day, we would sometimes be at home watching the news on the television, and something that we prayed for actually happened! It was so encouraging.

Of course, after we finished praying on Saturday mornings, we would go to eat something, like *nasi kucing*, an Indonesian food consisting of noodles mixed with very small fried fish. It's spicy and delicious and you can find it everywhere in Yogyakarta – especially late at night or very early in the morning – always wrapped in paper and sold at the street stalls. We could smell the chilli as soon we got out of the car. We loved it. That's how I got to know Linda, through praying.

So then, in 2011, I was back in Indonesia, and Linda and I began to pray and worship God together regularly again. At the end of that year, in December, we had a sense that we needed to meet more seriously and pray even more about the year to come. Both of us were really seeking God, wanting to realign our vision with his. We wanted to know what God wanted for us, for the year ahead. We were hungry to see more of God at work in our lives and we wanted to be radical Christians.

In the middle of December, we met together at Linda's house. She lived in Klaten, a forty-five-minute train trip east of Yogyakarta. As well as running their own school, Linda and her husband owned a distribution store. The basement of their house was like a warehouse. It was full of boxes. We prayed every day that week, and as we prayed, we had a sense that we were on the right track. But we wanted more. We wanted to bring more impact, and we wanted to see more of the Lord's harvest in Java, and also further afield in Indonesia and the world.

One night we went to their kitchen to pray. Linda's nephew was staying with them that week as well, and we didn't want to wake him up, so we went quietly to the kitchen. It was a huge area, part of the warehouse. We sat down on the tiled floor surrounded by boxes and we prayed. At first, all I could hear was a mouse scurrying in and out of the boxes near us. But then we held hands and began to worship God. I played the guitar. We were praying and longing for more of God.

Then God gave us both visions.

In my vision, I was taken up high, and I could see down from above. There was a huge harvest field.

I said to God, 'It's too high! Can you please take me closer to the field?' And he did. That's when I saw that the field was vast. It was full of wheat and it was ready for the harvest. The whole field was going yellow and it was starting to bend.

God said to me, 'The harvest is ready. It's the harvest that you are going to have.'

I replied, 'Wow! It's so big!' I couldn't even see the end of the field. It was filling up the whole horizon.

Then, after that, God took me to a room. Inside the room there was a long wooden table, and on the table there was a large fish.

God said to me, 'That fish is for you.'

'Really?' I responded. I didn't understand it at all. I kept looking at the fish on the table, and I kept repeating my question to God. 'Are you sure? Is it really for me?' In my spirit, I was so amazed. It was not just the size of the fish, it was more the sense that God would give me something so big. But God kept repeating it. 'That fish is for you,' he said. And as he said it, I became so happy in my spirit. The fish was for me. It was such a big fish! I still remember the feeling of great joy in my heart. I was stunned by the enormity of the harvest and by God's promise to me. It was such an unexpected gift. I felt overwhelmed. Somehow, God said that I was going to be a part of the harvest.

After some time in prayer, both Linda and I opened our eyes. Linda told me that she had seen a different vision. In her vision, she had seen a music scroll that the Lord had said was for her. We were both amazed as we shared with each other what we'd seen.

After that week, I went back home to Yogyakarta and I kept praying about the vision of the fish and the harvest. A week or so later, I began to search on the internet for pictures of big fish, and after a while, I found a fish that looked like the one that God had showed me in the vision. I printed it out and I put the picture on the wall above my desk. I started to pray over that picture of the fish. Sometime later, one of my other friends came to visit me. She saw the picture of the fish and she said, 'What is that fish on your wall?'

I told her about the vision that I had seen with Linda. Then she paused. 'Didn't you know?' she said, 'Catching a big fish means that you might be dating someone famous or marrying someone really important!'

I had never thought about that. I said, 'Really?' I just knew that the vision from God would come to fulfilment.

Linda and I kept praying. I prayed for the fish and Linda prayed for what she had seen.

A week or so later, in early January 2012, I received an email from my friend Eugen. Eugen and I had worked together in the church in Singapore and we had become good friends. Eugen was originally from Germany. He was involved with a local airline, and he was also visiting prisons in Indonesia with a prison ministry.

In the email, Eugen told me about a guy called Andrew Chan, one of the Bali Nine, who was in Kerobokan Prison. Eugen said that he had met Andrew in Bali while he was operating the flight from Hong Kong to Bali. He had visited Andrew in the prison.

At the time I received Eugen's email, I had never heard about the Bali Nine or about Andrew Chan. In the email, Eugen said that this guy, Andrew, wanted to build a prayer room at the prison so that people could come to pray. Apparently, Andrew needed someone to come to teach basic things to the inmates about prayer and worship. Eugen asked me if I could be that person. He knew that I was involved in prayer ministry in Yogyakarta and further afield in Indonesia and Singapore.

Back then, I had never been to a prison, and I didn't want to go to a prison. It wasn't something that I had ever thought about doing. I was also busy at that time. I was travelling to Singapore and around Indonesia for mission. I was still associated with the Singaporean church and I was also occasionally being sent to Malaysia. I was always sharing, and teaching local people in churches. We had a team, and we used to go together on mission trips. As well as teaching, I was also interpreting and translating for Indonesians in other countries.

So I didn't reply to Eugen. But every time I prayed, I got a sense that God was doing something new, and that he was about to speed up something and open a door. During that time, I began to wonder about this guy in prison. The prison was only in Bali; it wasn't that far from where I lived. Bali is only a ninety-minute flight from Yogyakarta and I had been there in the past. Perhaps I could make time to visit. But I was also scared. In Indonesia, I was doing many things as a pastor, ministering to all kinds of people – family, children and youth, even in dangerous places. It's what you have to do when you live in a small place. But I realised that the only ministry I hadn't been involved with was prison ministry.

My friend Eugen was persistent. He emailed again. This time he included a couple of links. He said that the links showed pictures, testimonies and stories in the news . . . all about Andrew Chan. But I didn't even open the links. I told him that I would pray about it.

That's when I rang Linda. We decided to pray and fast for three days in late January 2012. We went together up to a prayer mountain, in Yogyakarta. There is a place of prayer there, built on Mount Merapi, in the area of Kaliurang. The building itself consists of many small rooms designed for people who want to pray. The people come for free; they just want to pray.

We went there in Linda's car. It was the rainy season. When we arrived, we stayed on that prayer mountain for three days, and we prayed and fasted for many things. On the last day, before we came down, I remembered that I had promised Eugen I would pray for this man Andrew Chan. But I hadn't!

Our bags were already packed, but I said to Linda, 'Let's stop and pray for that man, Andrew.'

I wanted to know, should we go to Bali or not? Should I say yes to Eugen? We were both sitting in one of the small rooms. It was about 2 metres by 1 metre and the door was shut. There were people praying in the other rooms. Linda and I held hands and we began to pray for this guy, Andrew Chan. As soon as I said his name, we both suddenly felt a really strong wind begin to blow within the room. It began to blow everywhere in that small room, around and around us. It was crazy. We screamed and hugged each other. What was it? But in that moment, I knew that God was trying to tell me something. I slowly said, 'OK, Lord, I will go to Bali.' As soon as I said those words, the wind began to calm down. Then I heard the words, 'Go and set the captives free.' It was so clear in my mind. The words were from Isaiah 61. Linda heard the same words. Then the wind slowly stopped, and I heard a voice telling me to bring the anointing of the Holy Spirit to the prison.

After we opened our eyes, we both said, 'What was that?'

I said, 'Why would God want to send us to Kerobokan Prison, in Bali? Surely, he could choose someone from Bali, not Yogyakarta. There must be lots of pastors in Bali who could go and visit the prison.' But then, after a while, we both said that we should stop asking questions of God. We decided we should book our flights and go to Bali in June 2012. We had never been so sure of anything ever before.

I remember walking out of the place of prayer. It was 3 p.m. and we were due to break our fast. For the last three days, we had been praying and fasting all day in the small room and then breaking our fast at 3 p.m. Just outside the prayer house there was a large park to our right. The park was filled with green pine trees. It was hilly and beautiful. And right in front of the park, there was a street stall selling *wedang ronde jahe*. It's a deliciously hot ginger tea drink with rice and peanuts in it. It's especially good in the rainy season! So, on the third day, we sat down in the park and we drank *wedang ronde jahe*. The day was cold and wet, which meant that the ginger tasted even better. But I never smell or taste that tea now without remembering the utter conviction that we both had that we must visit Andrew Chan in Kerobokan Prison.

I went home and checked my emails. I opened the links that Eugen had sent me earlier, and I read some of the stories. By then, though, the video that Andrew had made of his testimony had been taken down. So I only read the public media items. I read that Andrew Chan was one of the Bali Nine. He was originally from Australia. Along with eight other people, Andrew had been arrested at Ngurah Rai International Airport in Denpasar, Bali, on 17 April 2005, for his significant involvement in a heroin drug smuggling operation. He was 21 at the time, and he had been named as one of the two ringleaders of the operation. Andrew went to prison, and ten months later, in February 2006, he was found guilty of drug trafficking. He was sentenced to execution by firing squad. Andrew had been in Kerobokan Prison ever since then, on death row. One of the links described Andrew's conversion to Christianity, shortly after his arrest. It said that Andrew was now active in pastoral ministry in Kerobokan Prison.

I looked at the photos that were taken of Andrew when he was arrested. His hair was dark and he seemed to be of Asian descent. He was quite skinny and there were tattoos on his arms.

I'm not a big fan of tattoos. I also saw that he had a scar on his forehead. I thought that he looked a bit scary, like a Chinese gang member. I had definitely never had a friend who looked like that.

I replied to Eugen and said that I would go to Bali to visit Andrew Chan.

4

He is Mighty to Save

*But when you pray, go into your room, close the
door and pray to your Father, who is unseen.
Then your Father, who sees what is done in se-
cret, will reward you.*

Matthew 6:6

I actually went to Kerobokan Prison, Bali, for the first time in
February 2012. It was only a few weeks after our time of prayer
on Mount Merapi. When Linda and I had gone home that
day, we both booked our flights to Bali for June, for the prayer
training in Kerobokan Prison. We were both really convinced
that it was God's will and plan for us. But I also went to Bali
for a holiday in February, just by myself. The holiday had been
pre-booked, prior to our prayer time on the mountain, and I
was due for a break from work. I had close friends living in the
city of Denpasar, which is west of Kuta Beach, Bali, and I had
stayed with them before, so I went there again on my holiday.

I must say, though, that I don't really find Bali an appealing
place. Many tourists visit Bali for holidays, but it doesn't feel like
home for me. It's not like Yogyakarta or Kupang. For starters,
the weather is very sticky. The humidity is much higher in Bali
than in Yogyakarta because it's closer to the beach. Also, Bali

is expensive. Sometimes, we would eat out in Bali for 50,000 rupiah (approx. 3 US dollars), whereas in Yogyakarta you could get the same meal for 20,000 rupiah. Bali is traditionally very Hindu. Every home in Bali has their own small shrine and there are Hindu temples everywhere on the streets, with marigold offerings all around them and the smell of incense in the air. It seeps into everything. Even the driving is different. The cars always push into your lane. The cafés are nice, though! They have amazing coffee.

So, I arrived in Bali in February 2012 and it was as sticky and chaotic as ever. I went to stay with my friends in Denpasar and we greeted each other as we normally did. But as I settled in and began to chat with them, I slowly began to wonder. Should I go to meet Andrew Chan by myself, while I was there in Bali? I was curious by then. And I was in the area. I knew that we needed to plan the teaching sessions for the prayer training in June, so I might as well go to see him and do the planning with him in person. I prayed about it and I asked the Lord if I should go. I had many questions. Should I go on my own as a single woman? What would the prison look like? What would Andrew be like? I was feeling a bit scared.

I decided to go. I contacted Andrew by email and told him that I was in Denpasar. Then I asked him if it was OK for me to visit him. He was surprised and said yes. He said that he loved visitors. Then he explained about the process of getting permission to visit. I borrowed my friend's motorbike, and I drove through the city to get to Kerobokan Prison. It was a forty-five-minute drive west of Denpasar, through the middle of the city, and closer to the beach.

I parked the motorbike outside the prison. From the car park, I looked up and I could see the high concrete walls and the barbed wire everywhere. I walked slowly towards the entrance. It felt very intimidating. There were so many guards and checkpoints.

It took quite a long time to get inside. The guards checked everything. I had to hand over my bag and everything I carried. The guards said that I could get my belongings back when I left. I felt very unsure of myself. Then a guy in charge of the visitors came to see me. He said that I had to have a number, and he took me to the visiting room. It was such a big room. He said that there had been a riot earlier that month and they needed to renovate the normal visiting area, so the prisoners were all gathered in the one room, sitting on the tiled floor. I stepped inside, and looked around. There were people sitting everywhere on the floor. I hated the feeling. It was so packed. Everyone was looking at me, as I came in by myself. I wanted to run away. I thought I had made a mistake.

Then the guy in charge of the visitors told me to sit down in a particular place, on the floor. There was no furniture at all. It was an empty hall. So I sat down on the hard floor and I waited. Where was Andrew? I prayed to God all the time, 'Please protect me.' I felt all alone. It was probably only fifteen minutes that I waited there, but it felt like forever. What was going to happen?

Then I heard a voice: 'Hey, how are you?' I could hear his Australian accent. There were a hundred people in the room, but I knew straight away it was him. I turned around and I saw his face. He was different to all the others. He seemed clean, easy to look at. Sometimes when you look at people, you can see if they're carrying burdens in their lives. But Andrew wasn't carrying burdens. He was easy-going. His voice was light. He was wearing a navy-blue basketball jersey and shorts. He had sunglasses on, but he took them off when he saw me.

We both said hello and we sat down and we talked and talked. I told him about what Eugen had said about the prayer ministry. Andrew said that it sounded great. Then he told me what he would like me to do in the prayer and worship training. He shared his vision for a place of prayer. Then he explained about how to write a letter to get permission from the warden. Then we both prayed for the training. We were still sitting on the floor, with people all around us, and we were both praying. It felt like a natural thing to do. Then, after we finished praying, I stood up and said goodbye to Andrew. Then I walked out of the prison. It was a relief to leave that place! But it was so good to see him. I knew he was different to the others. I could sense it straight away, and I felt I wanted to get to know him better. I wanted to know why he was different, even after seven years in one of the most notorious prisons in Indonesia. Why wasn't he burdened? Why didn't he carry a heavy heart, like the others?

After another week, I left my friends in Denpasar and returned to Yogyakarta. Andrew and I continued to email each other about the things we wanted to do in the prayer training. If I was going to visit the prison regularly, he said I had to go on the special list of visitors. Because Andrew was on death row, any visitor that wanted to see him needed special permission from the Australian embassy in Denpasar. There was a limit of ten people who could see Andrew every month, but Andrew could renew the list and make changes each month if he wished. So Andrew changed his registered list and he added my name; then we began to plan the training schedule for June. Andrew also went to the warden and asked for permission to run the prayer training programme. The warden gave us permission to do the teaching for three days, from 9 a.m. to 3 p.m., from the 27th to the 29th of June 2012. We decided that the course would be available to anyone in the prison, although we knew that mostly the Christians would come.

In late June 2012, I flew back to Bali and stayed with my friends in Denpasar again. This time, Linda came with me. Eugen had planned to come with us as well, but he had to change his schedule at the last minute, so Linda and I went on our own. Linda had also never been in a prison before and I remember that we were holding on to each other as we walked through the door. We were so nervous, slowly making our way to the chapel, which was past two checking points and beyond the maximum security area. We could see various inmates gathered in groups everywhere as we walked past maximum security. We kept walking. Then we saw the chapel on the right. It was a small yellow building and there was grass and flowers on the outside as well as a small blue baptismal pool. We went inside.

The chapel itself felt peaceful. The walls were white, and there were plastic chairs in the middle of the room and pictures of Jesus hanging on the walls. We had to be there before 9 a.m. to give us time to be checked through security. By the time we got to the chapel, some of the inmates had already gathered inside. Others were waiting outside in a line for the guards to give them permission to enter. On that first day, more than eighty people came – both men and women. The women's prison was next door to the men's, but the chapel was on the site of the men's prison, so the female inmates were escorted to the chapel under supervision. The guards mostly stayed outside, although some of them also came inside and listened.

Everybody was seated and ready, so we started a session on prayer. To begin with, we had fifteen minutes of prayer, praise and worship, led by Andrew. He went to the front and sang quite a few songs. Some of the other prisoners joined in.

I remember that Andrew closed his eyes when he sang 'Mighty to Save'. Later, I asked him where he had learned that song, and he said that he'd heard it on the internet, since being in prison. He liked the words. It was so true, he said. We all need compassion and we can trust in a God who is mighty to save – a God who can move the mountains.

Everyone needs compassion
A love that's never failing
Let mercy fall on me

Everyone needs forgiveness
The kindness of a Saviour
The hope of nations

Saviour, He can move the mountains
My God is mighty to save
He is mighty to save

Forever author of salvation
He rose and conquered the grave
Jesus conquered the grave

So take me as You find me
With all my fears and failures
Fill my life again

I give my life to follow
Everything I believe in
And now I surrender

Saviour, He can move the mountains
My God is mighty to save
He is mighty to save

Forever author of salvation
He rose and conquered the grave
Jesus conquered the grave

Shine your light and let the whole world see
We're singing for the glory of the risen King, Jesus . . .[1]

After the singing, Linda and I were feeling so blessed. We were amazed that these people in prison were worshipping Jesus more passionately than many people on the outside! Linda and I then introduced ourselves to the group and Linda shared for forty-five minutes about the grace of God. 'Why does God offer grace?' she asked. 'How can we feel accepted by God? How can we understand it?' She kept talking about forgiveness. 'God sent his perfect Son, the Lord Jesus, who lived and loved and taught the people and healed them and then died in their place,' she said. 'Jesus died for us. We have all done wrong things and we deserve punishment, but Jesus died in our place. He took the punishment we deserved so that we could be forgiven and be friends with God.'

All the people were listening intently. They were leaning forward. Then we had a break. We stopped and prayed for each other. We prayed that we (and they) could forgive ourselves and understand that God had forgiven us through Jesus. We prayed that we could forgive others and receive the grace of God.

It was the first day, and after it was finished, Linda and I went back to stay with my friends in Denpasar. We were both tired but we were also very encouraged, and by the second day, I was looking forward to it. I was starting to feel more comfortable. God was slowly changing me.

On the second day, Andrew began the programme by speaking about the father heart of God. He said that God loves us as his own children, and that God is a good Father. God would do anything to bring his own children back to himself, which is why he sent his Son, Jesus, to the world, to die for us and then to rise again. 'When Jesus rose from the dead,' Andrew explained, 'he broke the chains of sin and death for ever.' Andrew explained it so well, and he related everything to the message from the day before. Then after he finished, I walked to the front and I continued with the same theme. The people were sitting there, listening. The room was full.

Together, we read passages from Matthew, where Jesus talked about forgiveness and prayer. The great mercy of God is that we have been forgiven, through the death and resurrection of God's own Son, Jesus. None of us deserve it, but we can freely receive it. We can speak to God, in prayer, and we can know that he hears us. It doesn't matter about the words we use; we don't need to use fancy words or long, loud sentences. We can just call out to God and talk to him anytime, and he hears us, always. God knows us and loves us, and he wants us to come to him. He knows what we need, even before we ask him!

Together, we read out the prayer that Jesus prayed, from Matthew 6:9–13:

Our Father in heaven, hallowed be your name, your kingdom come, your will be done, on earth as it is in heaven. Give us today our daily bread. And forgive us our debts, as we also have forgiven our debtors. And lead us not into temptation, but deliver us from the evil one.

Then after we prayed, we had a ten-minute break. People were chatting to each other. They were really interested. After the break, we prayed for reconciliation between each of us and God. We led them in prayer and prayed for restoration. By then, most of the people were crying. None of them had ever had a good relationship with their parents. They hadn't had a good father. Most of them had been repeatedly abused. We kept praying for them and they joined in. Some of the people came up to the front for more prayer. We prayed that they would know God as their Father. It went on and on. I don't think anything like that had ever happened before in Kerobokan Prison.

Over those days, we saw that the training had begun to unite them to each other and to God. The people that week came from such different backgrounds, and they even came from different church denominations, so they had different opinions about how church should be run. But I said in the beginning that I didn't want to talk about denominations. I said that I wanted to talk about the Bible. I said to them, 'Do we agree first that we learn about prayer and worship from the Bible?' They all said yes. They agreed.

Then on the third day, there was even more of a breakthrough. At the start of the programme, I talked to them again about prayer. I asked them, 'What does the Bible say about prayer?' We talked about how we can listen to God's voice. We read what the Bible says about praise and worship, how to be a person of prayer and how to come to a house of prayer. We said that wherever we are, God hears us, even in a prison. It was the whole point of the training. It was the deepest thing on Andrew's heart. He wanted to start a prayer room.

On the last day, so many people were filled with the Spirit. They each started to hear the voice of God and they spoke in tongues – new languages given to them by God (as described in 1 Cor. 14). We told them to ask God, 'Do you love me?' And then they slowly shared with us what they would like prayer for. On that day, I realised that one of the Indonesian men had recently had a fight with an African guy. He hated the African and wanted to beat him up. But when they prayed that prayer at the end, I partnered those two men together. The Indonesian man started to cry and cry, and he hugged the African guy. They became good friends.

It was like a revival. After that, a lot of things changed in the prison. Firstly, they started to have cell groups (Bible study) in every block. There were eleven blocks in the prison, and for the first time, every block started a cell group. It was not easy to do that. It had never been done before – to have cell groups even in the most difficult, dangerous blocks. Before that, there was only a Bible study in one block – in the Christian block. You see, back then, the Christians would be put separately in one block and the Muslims in another, to make it easier. But suddenly, there were cell groups forming in every block. As well as that, once a week, Andrew would lead the English service and someone else would lead the Indonesian service. There were so many great testimonies during that time.

One man called Anton told us that he had been a leader in the Hindu religion in Bali. He was only young, but he had been teaching people about how to follow the Hindu religion for many years. Then he was caught and taken to police custody for a case of physical assault. He was sentenced to six months in Kerobokan Prison in 2012. But during those months in prison, Anton started to have dreams about Jesus. He didn't understand the dreams, so he began to look around and wonder who could help him. Somebody suggested that he go to talk to Andrew, so he did, and Andrew explained the gospel to him and led him to Christ. Later, Anton said that he was so changed. He admitted that he had been struggling before and that he couldn't control his anger. But then he would come to the cell group and share his struggles with the others, and he said that after a while, he stopped drinking and didn't smoke or take drugs any more. He said that even if someone provoked him or slapped him in the face, he was able to turn the other cheek because of Jesus (see Matt. 5:39). It was an amazing testimony to God's grace in his life.

All through that time, Andrew was praying for a larger house of prayer in the prison. It was his dream. He tried to plan for it. But in the meantime, the authorities set aside a small section of the chapel to be available for people to pray. They opened it all the time for anyone who wanted to pray, and the people began to come. They started to use it.

After that week in June came to an end, I was amazed. I said goodbye to Andrew and I went back home to Yogyakarta. But I kept in touch with Andrew via email almost every day. Most days, he would tell Linda and me what was happening in the prison and he asked us to pray for the cell groups and for the services each week. He told us about the needs of the prisoners. That's how our friendship developed. There were often people fighting in the prison, and he asked me to pray for them or for the sick people who didn't have any money to pay for treatment. We prayed together most days, via email.

Andrew's cell was in maximum high security, a separate block surrounded by its own fence within the prison. Every day, people would line up at the fence waiting to talk to him. They were always asking him for help, wanting him to pray for them. Often, he said, he would have three people waiting at the fence for him, at any one time. They called him Pastor. Every day, Andrew would go to a church service at 9 a.m., then go for exercise, then have lunch, and then do a Bible study outside with the men, under the tree outside one of the blocks. At the same time, the women would have their own Bible study groups on their side of the prison. Then Andrew would help more of the men who were struggling, have dinner and exercise, and after that, he would work on his Bible correspondence diploma course that he had begun through a Bible college in Melbourne. He had started it back in 2006, after he became a Christian. He studied hard every evening, and then at 8 p.m. he would contact me, every day, via email. It went on like that throughout 2012.

5

Faith as Small as a Mustard Seed

> *Truly I tell you, if you have faith as small as*
> *a mustard seed, you can say to this mountain,*
> *'Move from here to there,' and it will move.*
>   *Matthew 17:20*

One day, I asked Andrew about his own testimony. I wanted to know why he was not carrying burdens after seven years in prison. How had he become a Christian in prison? And how had he become a pastor to so many people in the prison?

Andrew told me that when he was arrested for drug smuggling, back in April 2005, he was in a bad way. He was taken straight to police custody in Denpasar. At that time, all he wanted to do was kill himself. He knew that he had done terrible things and that he had brought shame and suffering on his family and friends. All he could think about was how to hang himself. So, in that small cell, Andrew began to take his shirt off. He tried to work out how to make a noose with his shirt. He was in such a dark, despairing place. But then, as he sat there in custody, considering hanging himself, he also remembered some of the things that he'd heard about as a child.

Andrew grew up in Enfield, a suburb in inner-west Sydney, Australia. He had one brother and two older sisters. His parents were both first-generation immigrants from China. They were busy working in local restaurants. It meant that Andrew and his brother, Michael, in particular, had time on their hands. They became friends with their neighbours, the Sopers. The Sopers lived five doors down, in the same street, and the parents, David and Shelley Soper, were Salvation Army officers. David and Shelley's three sons, Luke, Joel and Mark, were close in age to Andrew and Michael. As the friendship developed between the two families, the Sopers would regularly invite the Chans to their Salvation Army church, as well as to their house for family get-togethers and on family holidays. It was during that time that Andrew first heard about Jesus and about heaven and hell.

Sitting there in custody in Denpasar, Andrew said that he began to pray and cry, 'Lord, if you are real, and if heaven is real, and if I die, I want to go to heaven to be with you.' He began to confess his sins to God. He knew that he was in a terrible place and that he had done terrible things. He had caused great suffering to many people, and he needed to ask for forgiveness. Then he said, 'Lord, if you are real, can you please send someone to help me. Please send them soon.' He was pleading with God, but at the back of his mind, he knew that it was impossible. He had only just been arrested, and he was certain that nobody else in the world knew about it yet. Then Andrew said that he blacked out. He didn't remember anything else.

The next thing that Andrew knew was that he woke up in his cell. It was 6.30 a.m. the next morning. He heard a guard banging on his door. The guard said, 'Get up. You have a visitor.'

Andrew stared at the door. He said, 'I can't have a visitor. Nobody knows that I'm here yet.'

Then the door opened and the visitor was his brother, Michael, and with him was Luke Soper. Andrew never expected a visitor – and he certainly didn't expect Luke or Michael! Andrew and Michael had gone their separate ways during their high school years, and they didn't have a good relationship at the time. Andrew had become involved with the wrong crowd as a teenager, and he had started dealing drugs as well as using them. He had become the ringleader of a drug smuggling operation. Surely, Michael would be the last person who would want to visit! And how had he come so quickly? For Andrew, it seemed like a miracle. God had sent Michael in answer to his prayer. They talked together, and then Luke Soper gave Andrew a Bible, suggesting that he read it.

Andrew said that he started to read the Bible as soon as they left. But, at first, it was hard for him to understand. It was a King James Version that Luke had picked up hurriedly on his way to the prison that day. Andrew began in Genesis, and he thought the stories were nice, but he didn't understand them or get anything out of it. So the next day, when Michael and Luke returned to visit, Andrew told Luke that he didn't understand the Bible. But Luke kept saying, 'Just keep reading; you will understand it later on.'

Andrew kept reading the Bible. About a week later, Luke returned to visit him and he gave Andrew a different version of the Bible that was easier for him to read and understand. Luke told him to start reading the Gospels. Andrew didn't know what the Gospels were, so Luke explained to him that they were about the life of Jesus, God's Son, and that the first Gospel was written by Jesus' disciple, Matthew. Andrew did as he was told. He read the Gospel of Matthew.

When he got up to chapter 17, he found a verse that later became one of his favourites. Jesus was talking to his disciples and he said, 'Truly I tell you, if you have faith as small as a mustard seed, you can say to this mountain, "Move from here to there," and it will move' (v. 20). Andrew said that he read that verse over and over again and he admitted that his understanding of God (and his faith) was very small . . . but he really wanted to know God, and he really wanted help. He wanted to be free. He wanted God to work in his life for good, so he said, 'God, if you are real, and if this is true, I want you to help me. I want you to free me . . . and if you do, I will serve you every day for the rest of my life.'

Nine months later, in February 2006, Andrew said that he went to his first court hearing, in Denpasar, hoping that God would free him. But at the trial, Andrew was found guilty of drug trafficking. He was deemed to be one of the two instigators and organisers of the whole operation, so he and the other man were sentenced to execution by firing squad; Andrew was given the death penalty. When he got back to his cell, he apparently said to God, 'I asked you to set me free, not kill me!'

Then God spoke powerfully to Andrew. He said, 'Andrew, I have set you free from the inside out. I have given you life!'

That was the moment that Andrew said everything changed for him. He understood the grace of God. Before that, Andrew said that he mostly wanted what he could get *out* of God, in terms of freedom from prison, but in that moment, he knew profoundly that he had been set free by God and given life 'to the full' (John 10:10), and for ever. He had been completely forgiven. He had not deserved anything good and yet he had received mercy from God.

From that moment on, Andrew said, he was changed. He didn't stop worshipping Jesus. He had never sung any song before; he couldn't actually sing in tune, but after that, he couldn't stop singing and praising God because Jesus had set him free. He also knew that his faith was still very small but that God was powerful and almighty, so he could do as he pleased with Andrew's life regardless of how many days Andrew had left on this earth.

That's how Andrew recounted his testimony to me, and he said that, over the years, he grew in his understanding. He really enjoyed his course through the Bible college in Melbourne. He had regular visits from the Sopers and from three other Christian families who lived in Australia, who took it in turns to visit Andrew in Bali – the Bairds, the Riddingtons and the Wilkinses. All of these families were there for Andrew whenever he needed them. If something happened in the prison, or with Andrew's case, they would be on the first flight to see him. They had a schedule between them and they took it in turns to be with Andrew, encouraging him in his faith and praying for him. They did it quietly, but they really cared for him. Over time, Andrew began to share his faith with the other prisoners; he counselled them and he prayed with them. Andrew became their pastor.

Talking with Andrew about his life and his faith encouraged me so much during those months in 2012. He always shared with me what was on his heart for the other prisoners. We kept praying together over email. Slowly, I decided that I would keep visiting the prison, and Andrew. It was clear that the direction was from God, so I planned visits in August, October and December that year. In the meantime, we kept in touch by email, and every day we shared what we had been reading in the Bible.

One time, I told Andrew that I had been reading John 21. In that passage, Jesus revealed himself to the disciples after his resurrection. He provided them with a miraculous catch of fish and then Jesus commissioned Peter. Jesus told Peter about the ministry he had for him in the years ahead. It was a unique and important calling for Peter, but then, straight away, Peter turned around and asked Jesus what would happen to the other disciple, John: 'Lord, what about him?' (v. 21). What would happen to John? It was a serious question for Peter, but Jesus actually scolded Peter for being a busybody. He said, 'If I want him [John] to remain alive until I return, what is that to you? You must follow me' (v. 22).

For me, it was a very challenging passage. It felt like God also scolded me through it. By then, I had occasionally been asking God what would happen to Andrew. Would he live or would he die? When would we know? What was going to happen with his death sentence? But the message I received from God, in that moment, was that the most important thing for me was that I followed Jesus. I didn't need to know what would happen to anyone else, including Andrew. Instead, God said, 'What is that to you? You must follow me!' It reminded me that God wants each of us to trust him and to do what he wants us to do, on the path he has marked out for us. We must each follow him not knowing what will happen to us or to anyone else. So I wrote all of this in an email to Andrew, as an encouragement, and he replied and said thank you. At the end of the email, I also reminded Andrew of the apostle Paul's words in Philippians 1, 'For to me, to live is Christ and to die is gain' (v. 21).

Ultimately, I said, it's the same for all of us, as we follow Jesus. We want to live for Christ, in all the time that he allows us on earth. Andrew agreed.

The next time that Linda and I went to visit the prison was in August 2012, and that time, Eugen came as well. We wanted the training to be a followup to the training in June. In the meantime, many other people had been coming to Christ and Andrew had baptised more and more of them in the baptismal pool outside the chapel. It was an exciting time. Eugen and the others taught the people about how to pray for healing. Along with them, another friend came to do some teaching for an extra two days. It felt like it was an intense time of prayer and renewal. Afterwards, I returned to Yogyakarta, but I kept having daily conversations and prayer with Andrew by email. Every day, we would share about what God was doing in our lives and in the prison.

One time, I remember, he told me about Jevry. Jevry had been a heroin addict and a drug dealer. He was in a really bad way. In prison, if you owe money to another prisoner for food, you can take your time to pay it back. But if you owe money for drugs, then it's not OK. Everybody gets angry about that, even if it's only small amounts of money owed. Jevry had a lot of debt to pay to people in prison because of his drug use. The due date for the money to be paid back was imminent, but Jevry had no money. So those other prisoners started to wait for him. They were the debt collectors and they were going to beat him up really badly. Jevry could be killed, because he owed so much money and the men were violent and angry.

He was really scared.

Jevry had started to attend one of the cell groups, so he went to see some of his friends to ask for help. The friends took him to see Andrew in the maximum high security block. They waited outside the fence to that block and asked the guards to send word that they wanted to see Andrew. Of course, in maximum high security, no one is allowed to go in or out without the approval of the guards, not even the other prisoners from the other blocks. The prisoners in maximum security are locked in their cells from 5 p.m. till 6.30 a.m. every day, but they can come out at other times. Jevry arrived at the fence and he sent word that he was looking for Andrew. The guards went to find Andrew and they did.

Andrew came out and took Jevry into maximum high security. When they got inside, the debt collectors couldn't go in. Instead, they waited in front of the fence. Inside, Andrew and Jevry talked and prayed for a very long time. Afterwards, they were able to go back out to the fence and talk to the debt collectors and negotiate with them. Andrew said, 'If you beat him up, you will not get the money. But give him time. We will talk to his family and friends to see if they can help him.'

Andrew was able to help Jevry. He talked to his friends. Everybody stayed calm. Andrew also contacted me and Linda and Eugen to pray for the situation, and we did. Jevry committed to stop using drugs, and he became Andrew's most trusted person and friend in prison. They talked every day and they read the Bible together.

Jevry was released after seven years and told everyone that it was Andrew who had helped him to have a different point of view. He said that he could see his life differently now. He knew that what he had done was wrong, but Jesus was able to change everything, even heroin addiction.

When Linda and I were back in Yogyakarta, in-between the prison visits to Bali, we started a prison ministry in Java in order to raise funds for the needs inside that prison. We kept visiting every few months. At the same time, I began to visit five other prisons in Java, including one on Nusa Kambangan, the seven-prison execution island west of Yogyakarta. By then, I had a deep heart for restoration in people's lives. I was getting to know the prisoners, and I realised that so many of them were second or third-time offenders. When they were released, they couldn't always go back to normal society. They were not accepted there. So, when they were released, they were often drawn back to the places where they *were* accepted – to their old communities and to their old patterns and lives. Every time I talked to the prisoners, they kept telling me the same story, and so, over time, we began to see the need for a safe house or a transit house in Java after they were released. Some of my friends were involved in setting this up.

I had another trip to Kerobokan in October and the ministry continued to grow. Then it was December 2012. I prayed with Linda again for the year ahead. I remember that she prayed for me, in particular for my life partner. She often did that at the end of the year, even though I didn't ask her to, and I myself didn't ever pray for a life partner. I said to her that I didn't want to get married. I wanted to focus on my full-time pastoral ministry. I had previously had a boyfriend, nine years earlier, when I was 23, but by December 2012, I was 32. I said I wasn't interested. But every year, Linda prayed for me. That year she prayed again for my life partner. As she prayed, she felt sure that the marriage I would have would be a marriage of vision.

She said, 'Feby, I've had a word from the Lord about your marriage. In your marriage, the shared vision will be the most important thing. It will be a marriage of vision and great joy.'

But then she said one other thing: 'When the two become one, it will be a marriage of great sacrifice and radical submission to God.'

6

The Children of Savu

Let the little children come to me, and do not
hinder them, for the kingdom of God belongs to
such as these.

Luke 18:16

The year 2013 was a busy one. Every day, Linda and I kept hearing about the prison ministry at Kerobokan and we shared the prayer needs with others. Many new things were happening in the prison. For example, one month Andrew had an idea to start a cooking ministry inside the prison, so we helped him to make contacts and we provided resources for him so that he could organise it and make it happen. After some time, he got permission to start a kitchen and began to hold cooking classes. Lots of people attended the classes, including a man called Ravi. Ravi said that he had been in the prison for several years, and that he had heard about the cooking class and went along because he really liked food. He thought it was going to be a party with lots and lots of food! But when he got there, Ravi met Andrew, and he thought that Andrew was different to the others. He wanted to know why. Then Ravi said that he tasted the food, and as he ate it, he had a longing for something more.

Ravi started going to the cell group in his block. The same thing happened there. He said that when he walked in to the room, he felt something different, and he slowly got to know the other people. He wanted what they had. He became quite emotional, and for the first time, Ravi admitted that his life was all wrong and he needed help. Then he watched Andrew playing his guitar and felt drawn into the song and the truths about Jesus. He wanted to keep listening and to play music himself and to learn the Bible.

It was funny because I had actually started to teach Andrew to play the guitar only a few months before that. I had taught him some simple chords to go with the worship songs that he liked to sing, such as 'Amazing Grace' and 'Mighty to Save'. Andrew learned the songs quickly, and he loved being able to play them on the guitar, in the chapel and by himself. When Ravi heard those songs as Andrew played them, he really wanted to know God. He prayed and prayed. Ravi soon became a blessing to the other prisoners.

It continued like that for those years. There was so much need in the prison. Kerobokan was designed to be a place for 300 prisoners and yet there were often 1,400 people at any one time. There were so many stories!

While Andrew was busily involved in the ministry at the prison, I knew that he was also praying and fasting about his own case. We didn't often talk about his case, or the details of it, mainly because there wasn't a lot of time. Whenever I visited the prison, we were busy in the ministry, and when I was back home in Yogyakarta, we were praying together over email and sharing about the needs of the other prisoners. So his case just didn't feel like the main thing, although I did know that Andrew had lost his second appeal back in May 2011. That decision had apparently been big news in Indonesia, as well as in other parts of the world, such as Australia. What it meant was that there was only one appeal left. I knew that Andrew's family and representatives were trying to stay calm and consider what to do before they reapplied for leniency, but Andrew himself didn't talk much about it. As I said above, we didn't have time! There was so much going on. There was a lot of counselling. Andrew was helping so many of the inmates, as well as the other prisoners' visitors.

I didn't ask him about the past. We enjoyed the present. I didn't even have the curiosity to ask him what exactly happened in 2005. Much later, someone asked me, 'How many kilograms of heroin did Andrew smuggle?' That's when I realised that I never asked him. I didn't know, and I didn't need to know, and we never talked about it.

While I was busy with the prison ministry, God began to put something brand new on my heart. God spoke to Linda and me about the small island of Savu. It was a very needy island, 1,300 kilometres east of Bali, and not far west from Kupang, in Timor. It was also a unique island. The population on the island was only 30,000, and although there had been some Christian evangelism in the past, the beliefs of most of the people were still heavily influenced by paganism, passed down through the generations to their children. For example, the people of Savu would regularly invite the devil, or the strong man (the *Orang Kuat*), to do something to another person or to make someone ill. So any time anyone became sick in a village, the first thing they would try to find out was whether it was black magic or witchcraft. If it was, they would ask the witchdoctor to come and do their business.

I knew quite a lot about the island of Savu because it was also the place where my father was born and raised until he was 10, before he moved to Kupang and met my mum. My dad would often talk about his childhood – walking to school on the island of Savu with no shoes on and playing with the other children. That's why, years later, he always told us to buy shoes half a size bigger, so that they would last. Shoes were such a precious item! Then, after my dad grew up and moved to Kupang, he often visited the island as an adult. One time, he took me with him. I was only young, but I remember visiting his relatives who still lived on the island and listening to them speaking Savunese together. I remember the feel of the sand beneath my feet and seeing such a lot of children.

In 2013, I told Linda about the island of Savu and the needs there. We also started to talk to my sister, who still lived in Kupang, and who was trained as a civil servant. She occasionally went to Savu for her work. As Linda and I began to pray about Savu, we became quite sure that God was going to do something wonderful there. We also shared the vision with Eugen. At that stage Eugen and his wife were involved with an outreach ministry associated with the well-known evangelist Reinhard Bonnke. So we prayed together, and we thought that maybe God would do a one-off, big evangelistic crusade on Savu, like in other parts of the world where Reinhard worked. It was an exciting thought.

Then, one day, in the middle of 2013, I went to visit Kerobokan Prison, and Andrew was praying and fasting for his case. He longed for God's hand in it. He said to me, 'Imagine if 1 million people could pray for my case, even for one minute each – what would God do?'

I agreed with him, and I shared his prayer concerns with many people back at home in Yogyakarta. I always asked for prayer for him and his case.

During that praying and fasting time in 2013, God also spoke to Andrew about reaching out to young people and children. Andrew told me about it during that visit, and he said that, at first, he didn't know if he had heard from God correctly because there were no young people or children in the prison. But then he thought that maybe it was because he was often talking to mothers in prison about their children.

Later, during that same visit, Andrew said, 'So tell me, what is God putting on your heart? What's happening with you?'

In reply, I shared with Andrew about what God had been saying to us about the island of Savu. I told him what God had said to me about the children and young people there. I explained that I really wanted to go to visit Savu. I also told Andrew that I had been there once when I was a child.

He said to me, 'Maybe this is the same vision.'

We still thought that we were going to have a crusade. I sent pictures of Savu to Linda, Eugen and Andrew. They were all so excited. We prayed for the preparations there and we thought about getting the churches involved. We wanted to go and see what was happening, to confirm why God had spoken to me about Savu.

At the end of 2013, I went to Savu. I flew from Yogyakarta to Bali, from Bali to Kupang and then from Kupang to Savu. It took me about seven hours in total. I remember getting off the plane, after seeing the whole island from the air. It was covered with little hills and coconut trees and palm trees. There were small houses with roofs made of palm trees. The people themselves looked quite a lot like my dad, with their sharp noses and dark skin. I kept looking at them because they reminded me so much of him.

I walked slowly from the airport. I could see that some of the people were eating *siri pinang* (betel nut) and wearing their traditional sarongs. But most of all, I noticed how many children there were. There were children everywhere, crowding around us, and playing outside the houses. That's when I realised that the ministry that we were going to have wasn't going to be a crusade. I was so sure that God wanted me to reach out to the children.

I still had relatives on Savu, through my father, so the first thing I did was to make my way to my uncle's house. He lived nearby in a village known as Raedewa. As I walked in that direction, I noticed that next to each house there were vegetables growing – spinach, cabbage, onion and chilli. Inside the houses I could see people cooking on firewood or on dried coconut leaves, using coconut shells to start the fires. Some of the houses had a kerosene burner. But they all told me later that the food tastes so much better if they cook it on coconut shells.

I found my uncle's village and his house, and everybody was very excited to see me. They all gave me the traditional nose-to-nose rub, which is the same on Savu as it is in Kupang. Actually, on Savu it's called the Savunese kiss and everybody does it, especially if you have been away for a long time. So they all kissed me nose-to-nose and then we sat down together on the front porch of my uncle's house. Savu is famous for its sugar made from the palm trees. They use it to make drinks and cakes. So we ate cakes and we drank coffee.

While we were sitting there, another man came up to us; he was the head of the village. He greeted me warmly and then he invited me to visit another village, which was not far away from my uncle's house. He was excited because apparently my father had visited that village six months before he died. Back then, my father had played the *Jesus* film at an event in the village. The *Jesus* film is about the life and teachings of Jesus, based on the Gospel of Luke, showing clearly that he is the Son of God. There had been a wonderful response and lots of people had come to Christ out of paganism.

I went with the head man, and when I arrived at the next village, the people were even more excited. They were all telling me about the film and thanking me that my father could come and share the good news about Jesus with them, back in 1994. As I sat there talking to that man, I noticed how many children there were everywhere, walking past us, playing, and so many teenagers. In my mind, the vision was growing. How could we reach out to all the children?

When I got back to Bali later that week, I shared the vision with Andrew and we started praying together about it. It's so hard to change the mindset of adults. But when you invest in children, it's easier for them to receive something new and good. For me to bring change to Indonesia, I knew that I needed to invest in the children. Perhaps we could build a community centre for the children on Savu?

7

For God's Glory

It is for God's glory so that God's Son may be glorified through it.

John 11:4

Something else happened at the end of 2013. It's hard to describe how it came about. By then, Andrew and I had been friends for almost two years. We had been sharing together most days and praying together for our concerns. We had been telling each other everything that was going on. Every month, we would cut ourselves off from other things and pray together. Our journey with God was very strong spiritually but not romantic at all. Whenever we met, he would hug me and give me a kiss on the cheek to say hello, but he did the same thing to everyone – and we were so involved in the ministry, helping people and praying for them. Back then, some of my friends occasionally said that they thought Andrew liked me in a special way, but I wasn't sure.

'How do you know?' I asked them.

'Because he always cooks really nice food for you!' they said.

In December 2013, Andrew contacted me to ask me if we could pray together. As we prayed, something new happened. Andrew prayed for our future together, and I prayed for our relationship together. It was the first time that we had mentioned it, or prayed like that, after being friends for all that time.

Before we talked, I knew that I admired him. I thought he was an amazing man of God, and I really liked him. I always looked forward to seeing him. He was so much fun! But I hadn't really considered what would happen if our feelings or our friendship became more serious. Slowly, though, during that prayer time, I started to think about him in a different way. We prayed for each other as if we were a couple. My friends asked me later. 'Did it come as a surprise . . . that thought of being in a relationship with Andrew?' It's a bit hard to say. I always wanted to be with him. We could talk about anything together and it was always so comfortable. I counted the days until I could see him again, and as we prayed together in December 2013, it felt right to pray for our relationship and for the way God could lead us and use us as a couple.

That same year, at Christmas, some of my family came with me to visit Andrew in Kerobokan Prison. They must have realised something had changed between us. I also began to think, 'This is real.' It hit me. Our relationship *was* becoming more serious. But Andrew was on death row. What would happen if he died? That thought came only for a short moment, though. I knew that I was committed to him. It was more than a shared vision and ministry. It was all of our life. We were talking as if we would spend the rest of our lives together. We were enjoying every moment and I believed that God could do a miracle in Andrew's life.

Christmas that year was fun. My mum and three of my sisters came with me. We all stayed together in a villa nearby, and we went to Kerobokan for Christmas Day. Andrew was chatty and fun, as he always was. It was so easy to get to know him.

Feby, her mum and two sisters at the airport.

Feby with her two sisters who prayed for her healing and led her to Christ.

Feby's whole family.

Feby with Linda in the van.

Feby at the prayer mountain.

The first time Feby saw Andrew preaching at the chapel in Kerobokan Prison.

Eugen, Feby and Andrew.

Andrew and Feby.

Looking down on the island of Savu.

Feby's parents on the
ferry to Savu.

Friends of Feby and Andrew, in Kerobokan Prison.

Andrew and Feby after a baptism at Kerobokan Prison.

Feby and Andrew's engagement.

Feby's last birthday with Andrew.

Roses for Feby's birthday.

Nusa Kambangan – Feby on the boat over to the prison.

Andrew and Feby's wedding day.

Feby holding Andrew's ashes with
Joe and Miranda Riddington.

Holding Andrew's ashes with Ann and Miranda.

Alan and Ann Wilkins next to Andrew's tombstone.

Feby, Linda and her husband at the opening of
Eden community centre, 2018.

Children playing at the community centre on
the island of Savu.

Every Christmas, the prison would allow special church services in an open area near the chapel, so that all the family
members of the prisoners could come and spend Christmas
together.

That year, there were hundreds of chairs outside and so many
Christmas lights draped around the space. Andrew cooked special food for us in the kitchen inside the maximum high security block. He prepared mashed potato, chicken and salad. We
sang carols together and we read from Luke 2 about the birth
of Jesus, and the way the angels sang, and the shepherds who
went to Bethlehem in a hurry to worship Jesus. The Saviour of
the world had come . . . and it was time to sing and worship
and celebrate!

At the end of the church service, we all sang 'We Wish You
a Merry Christmas', and everyone seemed relaxed and happy.
Some of the prisoners didn't have any visitors, but there were
other visitors who brought in extra gifts, and they distributed
them to the ones who had nothing, so everyone had something. My family told me afterwards that they were glad to be
there, and we took photos of us all together in the chapel.

It was a few weeks after that, in February 2014, that our
romantic relationship became official. It was public. We told
everyone that we were a couple, and it felt strange at first. I
remembered that some years earlier I had heard about someone
else dating a person on death row, and I had said, 'She must
be crazy!' And now it was me. But all the time I trusted that
God had sent me to meet Andrew, for a purpose. I knew that
for sure.

The more I prayed about our relationship together, the more
I felt sure that it was right. It was somehow part of God's plan. I
knew that Andrew wasn't a 'bad boy', as people suspected. That
wasn't part of the attraction. It was God's leading for me to be

in Kerobokan Prison, ministering with Andrew. There was so much confirmation, even from the beginning when Linda and I had prayed on Mount Merapi and felt the sudden wind. I had great faith in God. I knew that he could perform a miracle if he wanted to. I had seen so many miracles! I expected a miracle, and I was sure it would be Andrew's freedom. I never thought that he would die. In the meantime, we enjoyed the present. I enjoyed Andrew in every moment. I was so encouraged by him.

I also need to say that Andrew was not a saint. He was still learning and growing, as we all are. He was still figuring out his faith and how to be like Jesus in every moment. It was often hard. As well as being funny and friendly, Andrew could be sarcastic at times, without thinking. He was very quick and witty, but he was still learning how to rein in his tongue and to not let his words come out sounding mean. One time, there were people nearby making comments about Buddhist monks. They were saying how calm and patient the monks were. Andrew spoke up really quickly. He said, 'I'd be patient too, if I lived by myself, surrounded by no one! Tell the monks to come to prison, surrounded by people. Show me their patience then!'

Andrew would also often help people by cooking food for them. One time, though, he offered food to another inmate who happened to have Asperger syndrome. The other inmate thanked him but then commented that the food was cold.

Andrew replied very quickly, 'Yes, your majesty, there is no microwave. If you don't want it, give it back!'

It was his natural tendency to speak like that, and he knew he needed to work on his words, so we kept praying together, asking the Holy Spirit to continue to change us. It was part of our shared journey.

Also in 2014, I went back to the island of Savu. I began the next stage of the vision by surveying the government schools. I asked them what they would need most if I started a community centre. How could we help them? In reply to the survey, all the schools said that their students wanted to learn English and music, and they wanted a proper soccer field. None of those things existed or were available at any of the government schools on Savu.

So that's how it started. From then on, Andrew and I prayed for it to happen. During 2014, we developed the vision and the goals for a community centre on Savu, for the children. We made plans for the building. I visited twice more that year. We were about to build. Andrew linked people from around the world, talking about the vision. I talked to people on the island. The funny thing was that there wasn't a good signal on Savu, so I had to climb a tree to get the internet. There I would be, at the top of a tree, trying to get some signal and finding a way to pass on the information to Andrew, who was in prison in Bali, and he would then pass the information on to people further away, connecting them to the needs on Savu.

This was also the year that the picture of the big fish became clearer in my mind. Perhaps Andrew was the big fish, after all? We kept praying together, and we kept talking about the vision for Savu together. But still, at that stage, I wasn't thinking about the reality of marrying Andrew or how that might come about. When we talked, we talked about helping other people. I prayed for his friends. We both prayed for the vision for the community centre on Savu. We started a schedule of how to pray. We prayed for our family members on Tuesdays and Thursdays, and we prayed for our mission projects on Mondays and Wednesdays. The list of our prayer needs was getting longer and longer!

At the same time, the cell groups kept growing in the prison. We were looking for the right materials to help them, and each group had a slightly different focus or need. Andrew started to develop other ministries as well. He began to teach first aid to the inmates, as well as the cooking classes. He always wanted to help the other prisoners. The year went by very quickly. Every day, I looked forward to seeing him again. I couldn't wait to talk to him. It was always so comfortable, just to be with him. But there was always a lot of waiting.

When you arrive at Kerobokan Prison as a visitor, you take a number. Then you wait at the gate in a big crowd, and they call you in, one by one. Sometimes, it would feel like it was taking forever. Once inside, we would often only have one hour together. Every minute was precious, and Andrew tried to make it special. He knew that I liked it when he cooked, so he kept cooking special food for me and he would bring it into the visitors' area. Sometimes, he would cook meatball soup, or Vietnamese beef, or *pad thai*, or spaghetti. He would carry the food in from the little kitchen in maximum security, and then he would give it to me and we would both sit on the floor together in the visitors' area. The room was always packed with people, and there were no tables or chairs, so we would sit together on the floor, surrounded by people, eating Andrew's food. Sometimes, he would also bring a cushion for me to sit on. That was nice! Actually, it's hard for me to explain about how our relationship grew that year, but it did. We didn't have a lot of time on our own, and we couldn't go on a 'date' in the normal sense of the word, but I knew that I loved him and that he loved me, and that we always wanted to be together, somehow.

At the end of 2014, I began to think about moving long-term to Bali (in spite of the weather and the driving and the cost of a meal!). I thought it might be easier if I was closer to Andrew, so I didn't have to keep flying back and forth between

Yogyakarta and Bali. I wanted to be with him all the time! My friends in Denpasar were still happy for me to stay with them, whenever I came, which I did, but I started to think that it might be easier for me to relocate and find my own place in Bali. Perhaps I could work for the church there, and Andrew and I could spend more time together.

Our praying also changed that year. We often read John 11 together and we talked about the account of Lazarus. In that passage, Jesus heard that his friend Lazarus was ill, and at that point in the story, Jesus could have gone straight away to heal him, but he didn't. Jesus chose to stay where he was, for two more days, and then he explained it to his disciples: 'It is for God's glory so that God's Son may be glorified through it' (v. 4).

Everything that God does is for God's glory. Andrew and I kept reminding each other of that truth, and we kept saying that it was what we had to trust in, even during long times of waiting or when the things around us didn't make any sense at all.

As Andrew and I prayed together, we declared it. We said, 'Lord, whatever you are going to do in Andrew's life, please make your name glorified in this place, and in Indonesia, and in all the world.' We knew for sure that God could do it – that he could bring freedom for Andrew, any way he wanted.

But maybe the freedom that Andrew would get wouldn't necessarily be from the Indonesian government or from the Australian government. The freedom Andrew would get would be from God, and for God's glory, so we declared that. We kept praying together, every day, for God's glory in that situation, and in Kerobokan Prison, not knowing how he would bring it about.

8

Pray for Delay

The sun stopped in the middle of the sky and delayed going down about a full day.

Joshua 10:13

On 12 January 2015, it was Andrew's birthday. He was 31. I flew back to Bali again. I had never bought him a birthday present before, but that year, I gave him a watch for his present because I knew that he had broken his watch and needed a new one. I also brought him a cake. That particular day, there were quite a few other people around who knew it was Andrew's birthday, which was nice, but I remember that he tried to tell them not to come because he wanted to see me by myself! It was lovely. We had so much fun! I had never celebrated a boyfriend's birthday before. It made our relationship seem very real. We ate cake together and we sang songs and prayed together.

Back then, in the prison, the visitors were only allowed in from 9 a.m. to 11.30 a.m., but by the time you got past all the guards and security, it was often more like 10 a.m. or 10.30 a.m. by the time you were actually inside. So there was not much time! In the afternoon, the time slot was even shorter. But we enjoyed the time that we had that day.

By then, we had developed our own habits. Whenever we were sitting down together, he would hold my hand. He was such an excitable, friendly person. He knew everyone by name, and he would often call out or jump into conversations with people walking by. Occasionally, I would tell him that sometimes you need to let people talk first, and you need to learn to listen. So if I was holding his hand, we had our own signals. If I squeezed his hand twice, it was a sign that Andrew should stop and listen. And it worked. He actually paid attention to me. He was slowly learning to listen!

After Andrew's birthday, I went back to Yogyakarta for a week, and then I returned to Bali for the latter part of January and all of February. It was my birthday on the 19th February. I celebrated my 35th birthday in prison with Andrew. He arranged a birthday present for me – a bracelet. Some of his friends gave it to me on the outside, and then straight away, Andrew contacted me and said, 'Do you like your present?' I said I really liked it. I still wear it today. It was the last birthday we had together. But we had fun that day, and that month.

Up until then, Andrew had always liked to wear blue contact lenses and a big diamond earring. Most of his friends and family didn't like the lenses or the earring, and they tried to get him to stop wearing them, but he never did. Then, when we started dating, I didn't like the earring or the lenses either, but I couldn't tell him that. He had been through so much in prison. There were so many rules. You can't do this and you can't do that. I knew that if I told him that I didn't like the lenses or the earring, he would hate it. So I didn't tell him. Instead, I kept praying, 'Lord, what shall I do? How can I tell him about the lenses and the earring?' Finally, one day, I was supposed to come to meet him for church inside the chapel, but that day

Andrew happened to wake up late and had no time to put on his earring and his contact lenses. He went to church without them. I met him there and I thought he looked great! God reminded me to say something positive.

'Oh darling,' I said. 'You look so good today!'

'Really?' he said. 'What do you mean?'

I said, 'You look so manly without your accessories.' He just laughed and laughed. From that day on, he never wore the earring or the contact lenses again.

On another day, Andrew had had a difficult time. A lot of hard things had happened in the prison. But he sent me a photo, and I replied telling him that he looked so hot in the photo. He loved it. He laughed all day. It made him so happy. He had never heard me use the word 'hot' before. Then, after that, he would often wear the same white T-shirt that he had been wearing in the photo that he showed me.

At about that time, I told him about the vision that I had seen with Linda in December 2011. I told him about the harvest and about the big fish. He was amazed by the vision, and after a while he asked me if the fish that I had seen on the table was alive or dead. I was shocked. It had never crossed my mind. At first, I didn't know how to answer him. As I remembered the vision, I knew that the fish had not been moving. I knew that it was dead. But as I paused, I wondered what to tell Andrew. I didn't want to tell him that the fish was dead. Just in that moment, God told me what to say.

God said, 'Tell Andrew that whether the fish was alive or dead, it wasn't the most important thing. Tell him that you were really happy with the fish.' So I did. But while we were having fun and celebrating our birthdays together during those weeks, we also heard that Andrew's plea for clemency (the third appeal) had been rejected. The decision was made on

Thursday 22 January 2015 by the new president of Indonesia, Joko Widodo. I was shocked. I remember feeling broken. The news was everywhere, all over the media. I couldn't go anywhere without seeing it. There were all sorts of responses. But even then, in that moment, Andrew supported me. He hugged me. He said, 'Don't worry. God is in control. Jesus is in control. We still have time.'

After we heard the news, I contacted Linda on WhatsApp. We talked and we prayed together on the phone. As we did, a verse came to both of us, from Joshua 10. In that part of the Bible, the Israelites were fighting with their enemies and the Lord caused the sun to stand still. It says in verse 13: 'The sun stopped in the middle of the sky and delayed going down about a full day.'

We both thought that it was a strange verse to read, in relation to Andrew's case and the rejected appeal for clemency, but somehow we knew that we had to pray for 'delay'. We started to think that the execution would be delayed. God could bring about delay. We got the news of the rejected appeal (and the verse) midweek, and we prayed every day that week. The authorities had said, on the Thursday, that the plan was to transfer Andrew from Kerobokan to Nusa Kambangan (the execution island) that same weekend. We prayed and prayed and prayed. Then the news came that there had been a delay. Andrew couldn't be transferred that weekend. So we kept praying . . . and the transfer kept being delayed for six whole weeks, from the end of January until the first week in March. During that time, we spread the word to everyone. Pray for delay, we said! It became the prayer that everyone was praying for, even all the prisoners in Kerobokan – Anton, Jevry and Ravi – and all the others around the world. They were praying for Andrew and his case. We trusted that God would hold the delay for his purposes and that it would give us time to fight.

I remember that Andrew preached about that passage in Joshua at the chapel in early February. That same month, he had been ordained as a minister of the Word, having one final subject to go in his Bible course through the Bible college in Melbourne. Andrew stood up and he spoke to all the people who were sitting there in the chapel that day.

'I don't know how God stopped the sun back in the time of Joshua,' he said, 'and I don't need to know; in my case, I don't know how God is going to send the delay in my execution or what his purposes are . . . but I trust him for it. I know that all of time belongs to him.'

Then, together, we all stood up in the chapel and we sang 'Amazing Grace', one of Andrew's favourite songs.

Amazing grace! How sweet the sound
That saved a wretch like me!
I once was lost, but now am found;
Was blind, but now I see.

'Twas grace that taught my heart to fear,
And grace my fears relieved;
How precious did that grace appear
The hour I first believed!

Through many dangers, toils and snares,
I have already come;
'Tis grace hath brought me safe thus far,
And grace will lead me home.

The Lord has promised good to me,
His Word my hope secures;
He will my shield and portion be,
As long as life endures.

When we've been there ten thousand years,
Bright shining as the sun,
We've no less days to sing God's praise
Than when we'd first begun.

John Newton (1725–1807)
Amazing Grace, vv. 1–4,7, Cyber Hymnal™ http://www.hymntime.
com/tch/htm/a/m/a/z/amazing_grace.htm (accessed 27 October
2020).

I remained there in Bali, staying with my friends in Denpasar,
until the 3rd March. I kept visiting Andrew every day in
Kerobokan Prison. We kept ministering together and praying together. More and more people came to the chapel services. Then on the 3rd March, we heard that Andrew would be
taken from Kerobokan Prison to Besi Prison on the execution
island – Nusa Kambangan.

The same week, I received a text from an Indonesian pastor
friend of mine who had a large network of people who prayed
regularly. He said that he had just sent out an email to all his
contacts, all over Indonesia and Asia. He had asked each of
them to pray for Andrew for one minute each. He told me that
there were 1 million email addresses. It was amazing. It was
exactly what Andrew had prayed for, nearly two years earlier.
Andrew had said, 'Imagine if 1 million people could pray for
my case, even for one minute each – what would God do?'

9

On Nusa Kambangan

But I have prayed for you . . . that your faith
may not fail.

Luke 22:32

When they transferred Andrew from Kerobokan Prison to
Nusa Kambangan Island, they took him to the airport in a military tank. Inside the tank and surrounding the tank there were
army soldiers. There were soldiers everywhere that day. We
were on the outside, watching as they put Andrew in the tank.
I remember feeling shocked. How could they treat Andrew like
that? What did they think he was going to do? He wasn't a
dangerous terrorist! But Andrew told me later that when he
got inside the tank, he didn't mind at all. He was just enjoying
looking out of the small window, enjoying the view for the first
time in ten years. He was making funny comments about the
trees that he could see and the houses and buildings. He hadn't
seen a view like that for so long. He was enjoying it and taking
it easy while, on the outside, we were all so worried about him!

It took five days for the authorities to settle Andrew onto the
execution island at Nusa Kambangan and make sure everything
was secure. Then I was allowed to visit him in Besi Prison.
There are seven different prisons on Nusa Kambangan Island.

All of them are maximum security and reserved for the worst cases, like terrorism. The whole island is only for prisoners. To get there, I had to fly back to Yogyakarta, in Central Java, and then drive for five hours to the south of Java, near the coastal town of Cilacap.

I remember that day; when I arrived in Cilacap, there was a strict security check, and then I took a boat from Cilacap across the water to the island. On the other side of the water, there was a car to take the visitors to the prison, and then there was more security. It took a whole day to get inside. The island was a jungle. They told us that there were tigers in the jungle and wild cats. The security seemed worse to me than the thought of tigers. It was so tense the way they checked me. It felt tormenting – every time. They questioned me again and again, even when they knew who I was, and even though I went there so often. Back in Kerobokan Prison, I used to be able to visit Andrew every day that I was there, especially for the final six weeks, but on that island, you could only visit inmates on Mondays and Wednesdays; so I booked into a hotel in Cilacap and stayed there from Monday till Wednesday, visiting Andrew, and then I went back home to Yogyakarta on Thursday. I came back to Cilacap again on Sunday, and I did it all over again, for seven weeks.

Going back to Yogyakarta on Thursdays, I was so tired. I just needed to rest. The hardest thing was that there was no other form of communication with Andrew in-between the visits. There was no internet. I wrote letters to Andrew every day, and I took them with me on Mondays. I gave the letters to the guards on the way in and I knew they screened everything. So I wrote to him about what I had been doing, every hour of the day. Andrew wrote letters back to me, every day, and the guards gave me his letters on my way out. But Andrew couldn't write anything about the prison, because of the screening. Instead, he wrote about the books he'd been reading. Sometimes he would write about Savu and our shared vision.

'Oh, *Sayang*,' (Darling), he would write, 'you need to go back to Savu to dig the well, so that we can have enough water for when we start the centre for the children.' He would discuss it all with me. He knew that there was a water problem on Savu. At other times, he would write to me about the things that he'd seen on the island – the eagles that were flying around above him or the wild cats that would come to visit.

On the days when I was back in Yogyakarta, I was also busy fielding questions. Some of my family members were calling me or sending me texts asking, 'Why are you seeing someone on death row?' It was all over the media, and my family were very private people. They worked with the government, so there were strict guidelines about not being involved in the media. It was understandable and very sensitive. People nearby were asking them what was going on with me and Andrew, and they couldn't say anything. It was very hard.

I remember the time in 2014 when I told my mother everything about me and Andrew. I didn't want her to find out from other people. She kept quiet. Then she said, 'Feby, since you were young, I could see God's hand in your life. I prayed for it. And I know that you belong to God. I have already released you to him. So I trust God for your life, and I know that you have prayed about this.'

She also said that it was very hard for her, as a mother, and I could understand her point of view. She wanted the best for me and she loved me. She didn't want me to be hurt. Linda was the same. She understood, and she knew about the vision I'd seen of the big fish, but she was still sad for me because she knew that I would be hurt – and she knew that I would be obedient to God.

It went on like that for seven weeks. Andrew told me that the hardest part was not being able to communicate with anyone during the day. He was in an isolation room for twenty-three hours each day. It was maximum high security. It was the death sentence. Before that, Andrew had been so busy with other people, always counselling them or helping them or praying with them. The inmates were always lining up for Andrew outside the fence in Kerobokan. And now there was nobody. I can't imagine how hard it was for someone like him, in isolation. He got his energy from other people.

During that time in isolation, he asked me to bring him books, and I did. I brought Christian biographies and other Christian books. For those seven weeks, Andrew just read and prayed and wrote letters.

He wrote a letter to his little nephew. Andrew had only met him once, in Kerobokan Prison earlier that year, when his eldest sister came to visit him, bringing her child. Andrew loved his nephew straight away. He hugged him and played with him. So, during his time on Nusa Kambangan, Andrew wrote a letter to his nephew. He said, 'I wish I could have spent more time with you and taken you to footy games. I would have made you a Penrith Panthers fan! And I would have told you all about Jesus. I love you . . . keep looking to Jesus, trust in his ways and learn from my mistakes.'

To go to visit the prison on Nusa Kambangan, you needed to get permission from the high court. We scheduled people from his family and network to go with me, each week, for seven weeks. They allowed us to sit on the porch in front of the office. The guards were all around us. But once I was inside, past all the security checks, I didn't have that same scary feeling. I didn't see the other prisoners. I just saw Andrew. Every time, when I saw him walking towards me, I just felt joy. I could see his face and I knew he was so happy to see me. We didn't talk about what was about to happen.

There were things that made us laugh. Andrew had started to learn Javanese so that he could chat with the guards on the island – just numbers and simple greetings. When he was in Kerobokan Prison, he had learned Balinese, but the people on Nusa Kambangan didn't understand Balinese, so that's why he began to learn Javanese. One day I came to visit and there was a friendly guard nearby. He greeted Andrew in Javanese and Andrew replied in Javanese. I was shocked! I said, 'How did you learn Javanese in such a short time?' Andrew laughed with me. Then he spoke it whenever he could. He would say things in Javanese like, 'Have you eaten today?'

All the guards liked him. There was one guard who never wore socks. Andrew kept asking him, 'Why don't you wear socks? Do you want me to get you some socks?'

But the guard would always reply, 'No, thanks. It's too hot to wear socks!'

Another time while I was visiting, a female guard passed by. She was always friendly. This time, Andrew asked her about another guard – who was male and single. He was trying to do some matchmaking while he was there. They both laughed with him. They loved him. He was funny and friendly to everyone.

In those weeks, some of the wild cats in the jungle would also come to visit near Andrew's cell. There was one cat in particular who became quite friendly and would often visit. Andrew knew the cat, and the cat knew him. One day, Andrew put his sunglasses on the cat's face. He asked the guards, 'What is the cat's name?'

The guards tried to guess the cat's name but they couldn't get it right.

Then Andrew said, 'It's the guard over there!' He pointed at one of the guards and there was definitely a likeness. Everyone laughed.

The guards told Andrew, 'You naughty boy!' and then they warned the others: 'He will make fun of you!'

They were very strict about time in that prison, particularly the time the prisoners could go out for their one-hour break in the 24-hour period, and the time they had to be locked back in. Everything was written down in a book. Every thirty minutes, the guards would document what the prisoners were doing. One day, it was time for their one-hour break. Andrew was inside his cell and he reminded his guard of the time, but the guard put him off. The guard looked at his watch and he said that it would be another fifteen minutes. It happened three times. Finally the guard unlocked the door. The guard needed to use the toilet, so he went into Andrew's cell and used his. While he was doing that, Andrew went outside and locked the guard in! The other guards were all watching and they thought it was funny. They were laughing and they let it happen. Then Andrew sat down on the guard's chair, and he pretended to look at his watch. He said to the guard, 'Now, I'm afraid we have to wait for another fifteen minutes . . .'

They loved him because he was funny.

One day, Andrew said to me, '*Sayang*, can you see the difference? I've lost 7 kilograms.'

I smiled and agreed with him. I knew that he'd lost weight. He'd been fasting and praying, as well as cutting out sugar and soft drinks. So I said, 'Yeah, honey, you look amazing!'

Andrew loved fruit, especially *duku*. *Duku* is a fruit that is a little bit like a lychee. And it just so happened that during

March and April, it was the season for *duku*. So one time when I couldn't visit Andrew, I sent him a whole bag of *duku*, via his mother. He wrote back, '*Sayang*, I was so happy! I saw the *duku* and I knew it was from you. Nobody else knows how much I like *duku*!' He knew that I had paid attention to what he liked.

Then, Andrew would also ask me what was happening in my life. He would want to know everything that I'd been doing. But mostly, I would tell him funny stories. All I could think about was him. How could I help him to stay strong in his faith in Jesus? It was the only thing on my mind. I couldn't even cry. If I cried, it would just break him. So I kept smiling. That's why I didn't think about what was about to happen. I knew that I needed to be strong for him. Also, I didn't want fear to come in and disturb my faith or his faith. I didn't want our faith to fail.

I still believed for all those weeks that God would do a miracle. God would bring Andrew freedom.

10

I Said Yes

Suppose one of you wants to build a tower. Won't you first sit down and estimate the cost to see if you have enough money to complete it?

Luke 14:28

At the beginning of Andrew's time on Nusa Kambangan, on 3 March 2015, it was only Andrew and two other prisoners on death row who had been brought to the island for execution by firing squad. But gradually a few other people were also brought in from different prisons. They were gathering them, and by mid-April, they were all there together. We got the feeling that something was about to happen. But during all that time, Andrew told me that, whenever he could, he took the others on death row aside and he prayed with them. Every morning they worshipped God together and had communion together, and they prayed for the guards who were watching them. One day when I went to visit, Andrew came out to see me and his face was glowing. I wondered why it was glowing so much. He said that one of the other prisoners had finally given his life to the Lord.

It was the greatest miracle of the whole time. That person had always been making fun of Andrew's faith. But in the end, the person said that his decision hadn't come because he was on death row. He said that he had finally made peace with God. Andrew was delighted.

The day before, we had been talking about one of Andrew's favourite verses in the Bible.

> Truly I tell you, if you have faith as small as a mustard seed, you can say to this mountain, 'Move from here to there,' and it will move.
>
> *Matthew 17:20*

Andrew continued to believe that with all his heart, and we kept praying for the Lord's work in that prison on the execution island, among the prisoners and the guards.

Somehow, after that prisoner came to the Lord, it was as if God said, 'It's done.' God had done what he was planning to do. Afterwards, we wondered whether that was why the execution was delayed. Andrew had been praying every morning, 'Please send me to the person I can talk to today, about you.' The person who responded that day was one of the eight prisoners about to be executed – the one who Andrew had been praying for and sharing with, the whole time. How precious is that one person to God?

Then, suddenly, the 72-hour countdown to execution was announced.

On Saturday 25 April 2015, I was in the hotel in Cilacap with a couple of family members of one of the other prisoners. It was about 4 o'clock in the afternoon, and we overheard something. An official from an embassy went up to the family group of another prisoner, and they told them that the 72-hour countdown had been announced. The prisoners were going to be executed.

We heard it indirectly, while we were sitting there in the hotel – not from Andrew's lawyers or from the embassy. I started to shake. We knew that there had been a meeting and the government had called the embassies from the other countries to come to Nusa Kambangan. We suspected that they called them so that the news wouldn't leak out. But in the end, I overheard it.

I couldn't stop shaking. We were still hoping for a miracle. The announcement of the seventy-two hours meant that security was tightened up, and the prisoners were 'sterilised'. The term refers to the restriction of their normal activities as the execution had become imminent. There were police everywhere. It was crazy. The authorities knew that once the media found out, every country would react. But I kept telling myself that I still believed in miracles.

The hardest part was that I couldn't talk to Andrew. I couldn't find out how he was doing. I couldn't pray with him. I was panicking. I wanted to know how he was. Were they treating him well? It was a battle in my mind. I sat down. I said, 'I still believe in you, Jesus, I still trust in you. I still believe you can do miracles, even to the last minute.'

We were allowed to visit him the next morning. I was with a group of Andrew's close friends and family members. It was a Sunday. I walked through the door and I saw Andrew walking towards me. It was the first time that I had seen him in handcuffs and chains. I was shocked. Thankfully, I had my scarf with me. I couldn't hold back my tears. I cried like crazy. He tried to hug me but it was so hard with the handcuffs on. I covered my face and I cried and cried. The guards came and saw me. They said that they could undo the handcuffs so that Andrew could hug me, and they did. I didn't expect that. It was the only time I cried. It was so sad. But even that day, Andrew was still able to calm me down. He said, 'Baby, it's OK. Jesus is still in control. Look up to him.'

Then the guards took the chains off Andrew. They realised that they didn't need them. The day before, on the Saturday, the government had asked Andrew if he had three last wishes. He said yes, he did. He said that he wanted to contact his father and his sisters in Sydney, who hadn't been able to come over and visit him while he was on Nusa Kambangan. Then he said that he wanted to pray with his visiting friends and family, one last time, in the prison chapel.

When I went in the afternoon, we talked together. He told me about his last wishes and that we would be able to go to the chapel the next day to pray. Then he said to me, 'Do you want to go to the chapel by ourselves, just the two of us?'

'The two of us?' I said. 'Don't you want your family there?'

He smiled and then he said, 'Would you like to get married?'

It wasn't a surprise. Andrew had already proposed to me, back in Kerobokan Prison, on the 12th February that year.

After his clemency was rejected in January, there had been a new rule that said that Andrew couldn't sit in the common visiting area with the others. It was mainly because there were so many people trying to take photos of Andrew to sell to the media. So they put Andrew in the main hall, at the back of the prison, and if anyone wanted to visit him, we had to go there. The good thing was that the main hall was more private than the common visiting area. Nobody else was there, except for Andrew and his family and friends. Mind you, there were also wild cats there and they left a smell.

That particular afternoon, back on 12 February 2015, the rest of Andrew's visitors had gone out to lunch. Andrew asked them to please not come back for a while. As well as that, he asked for permission from the authorities for me to stay back and have lunch with him, in the prison. The authorities said yes, and so I stayed with him. It was the only time I was ever allowed to have lunch with Andrew, by ourselves, in Kerobokan Prison. I remember that it was so hot in the hall, though. I was fanning my face with my hands, and the smell of the wild cats was all around us. There were also guards outside, watching us through the windows.

Then Andrew said to me, 'Can you just stay here for a moment? I have to go to my room.'

I wondered what he was doing. I sat in the hall by myself and then, when he came back, he asked me if I would like to take a tour of the prison with him. I said yes. It was a little bit strange. He showed me everything – the different blocks, the chapel and the halls. He pointed them all out.

Then we went back inside the main hall and he said, 'Do you want to marry me?'

I said, 'Yes, of course I do!' Then I paused. 'Do you mean right now?'

He said, 'No, not right now. But do you want to marry me?'

I said, 'Of course I do.'

Then he took out a ring from his pocket and he gave it to me. It was beautiful. It had four diamonds in a square.

He looked at me and said, 'Do you want me to kneel down?'

I laughed and said, 'No, the guards would see!'

Then, after that, his other visitors started to come back after their lunch. Andrew told them that he had proposed to me. He was so happy. I showed them the ring and they all said, 'Oh, congratulations!' They even brought us a cake, the next day, to celebrate. But we couldn't get married during those remaining weeks in Bali. Andrew asked his representatives for permission and they said no. They said that it would inflame the situation and we needed to avoid anything that would do that. We needed to keep everything calm.

So there we were on Nusa Kambangan, on the 26th April, after the seventy-two hours were announced, and Andrew asked me to marry him, again. It was his third wish.

I said, 'The media will find out.'

He said, 'Yes, they might. That's why it could be just the two of us, without anyone knowing.'

I said, 'But don't you want your family there?'

He said, 'Yes, I do. I just want to avoid the media.'

I said, 'OK' – I agreed with him. We both wanted to avoid the media and we knew the news of our wedding would get out. But I said yes to his proposal. I had already said yes, back in Kerobokan.

I didn't tell anyone after that, though. I didn't think anyone else knew – only Andrew and me, and Andrew's spiritual advisor, David Soper, who had also come to Nusa Kambangan to be with Andrew at the end. I went back to my hotel room in Cilacap. I started to pray. As I prayed about what to do, God reminded me of the verse in Luke 14 where Jesus was talking to the crowds about the cost of being a disciple. He said that it would be hard for them to follow him. Then Jesus also said, 'Suppose one of you wants to build a tower. Won't you first sit down and estimate the cost to see if you have enough money to complete it?' (v. 28).

It was a helpful reminder for me to stop and plan and estimate, as well as to pray earnestly. So I sat down and I wrote a list on a piece of paper. What would happen if I married Andrew? What would happen if I didn't? I had two columns and I wrote down many things, on both sides. On the one hand, I knew that if I married Andrew, I would have a mark on myself. I would have married an ex-drug trafficker. His story would be linked with mine for the rest of my life. People would think that I was crazy. They would assume all sorts of things about me and him. They would question my motives. But if I didn't marry him, would I live with regret? Would I wish that I had married him? But mostly, I thought about Andrew. Would it be a source of strength for him? Was this what he wanted? Would it help his faith to remain strong? Would it help him in the end? I wrote everything down on my lists.

Then I prayed. I said to God, 'Lord, I know that you are in control. You can do what you want with our lives. If you don't want this wedding, you can stop it.'

With the announcement of the seventy-two hours, Andrew couldn't even change his clothes. He was under the full control of the prison and the high court of Indonesia. The approval for a marriage would have to come from Indonesia's Attorney General – and it was easy for someone like the Attorney General to simply say no. He could just say that it would be too much trouble. It seemed the most likely outcome. But more than that, I said to God, 'Lord, please give me peace about it, tomorrow. Please show me what you want me to do.'

There were also two of Andrew's family friends staying with us at the hotel – Alan and Ann Wilkins. So I told them about our plans for the next day and I asked Alan if he would like to walk me down the aisle. Both Alan and Ann had been like second parents for Andrew, ever since he had been in prison.

Alan said that he would walk me down the aisle.

11

Bless the Lord, O My Soul

Sing to the LORD a new song; sing to the LORD,
all the earth. Sing to the LORD, praise his name;
proclaim his salvation day after day.
Psalm 96:1,2

The next morning I woke up with peace. I had such a calm mind. I got dressed slowly and I made myself ready. We went as a group to the port in Cilacap and then we got on the boat to cross the water.

We arrived at the other side and stopped at the checking point. That's when we found out. The Attorney General of Indonesia had said yes. He had allowed the wedding. We walked to the car and got in and drove to the prison.

Just outside Besi Prison, there was a bougainvillea in full flower. It was a beautiful dark pink/orange colour. One of our close friends and supporters quietly stopped and picked some flowers, and I put them in my bag. I might need a bouquet.

Andrew was so happy when he saw me. He had such a big smile. He told me that the head warden of the prison had also allowed the wedding. We went into the chapel; there were ten of us, including Andrew's brother, Michael, and his mother, Helen. Alan walked me in. Andrew was inside, waiting for me, and David Soper was up the front, ready to marry us. We stood there and we sang 'Amazing Grace' together. We prayed. Then we sang '10,000 Reasons'. It wasn't hard to sing. It helped me. I could worship God. I knew as I sang that it was true: I would bless the Lord no matter what happened, and I knew that we both wanted to bring glory to God. That was the main thing, from the beginning of our relationship until the end. We both wanted to point to Jesus and to sing his praises. So we sang:

Bless the Lord O my soul
O my soul
Worship His Holy name
Sing like never before
O my soul
I'll worship Your Holy name

The sun comes up
It's a new day dawning
It's time to sing Your song again
Whatever may pass
And whatever lies before me
Let me be singing
When the evening comes

Bless the Lord O my soul
O my soul
Worship His Holy name
Sing like never before
O my soul
I'll worship Your Holy name

You're rich in love
And You're slow to anger
Your name is great
And Your heart is kind
For all Your goodness
I will keep on singing
Ten thousand reasons
For my heart to find

Bless the Lord O my soul
O my soul
Worship His Holy name
Sing like never before
O my soul
I'll worship Your Holy name
Bless You Lord

And on that day
When my strength is failing
The end draws near
And my time has come
Still my soul will
Sing Your praise unending
Ten thousand years
And then forevermore
Forevermore[2]

Then we said our vows to each other. I had stayed up all night thinking about my vows. I didn't know what to say. I didn't want to say, 'Till death do us part.' What if it was the next day?

So I said to Andrew, 'In front of God, whatever might happen after this, I will stay by your side, even if I have to take the bullet with you.'

Andrew replied, 'As long as I am alive, I am not going to let you do that!' Then he said his vows to me. He said, 'I thought that love would have a limit. But with you, my love for you goes on and on. It has no limit. You bring out the best in me. You bring out the gold.' Then he paused and I repeated the words back to him. I felt the same thing. He was so happy. I can remember the look on his face. His smile was so big!

Our decision to get married had happened so quickly that we hadn't had time to organise rings. So that morning, David Soper was thinking about the rings. He hadn't taken his own wedding ring off in about forty years. It was stuck on his hand! But that morning he prayed, 'Lord, if you want me to take my ring off and give it to Andrew, please let it come off.' And it did – the ring came off!

When David arrived at the chapel that morning, he showed his ring to Andrew and it fitted perfectly. It was not too tight and it was not too loose. David led us as we exchanged rings. Andrew gave me the ring that he had given me for our engagement, and I gave him the ring from David. Then David pronounced us man and wife.

At the end of the service, Andrew led the closing prayer. He said to God, very simply, 'Thank you, God, for today. Thank you for Feby. Thank you for everything. Amen.' Then the guard took a photo of us. When I look at it now, I notice that none of us were wearing shoes. Being in a prison, the visitors weren't allowed to wear shoes or socks because we could have hidden things in our shoes. So we were all in bare feet, inside the chapel. Only Andrew was wearing shoes!

Afterwards, we walked out together from the chapel into the visiting area and everyone, the whole prison, was clapping and cheering us. All the other prisoners' family members were clapping. Only ten of us had been allowed into the chapel, but outside everyone knew.

We sat down together. All Andrew wanted was for me to sit on his lap, so I did. I stayed there all afternoon, from 2 p.m. until 5 p.m. The whole time, I was worried that he might be getting tired with me on his lap, but he kept saying that he didn't want me to move. At the end, they gave me forty-five minutes alone with him, so we could say whatever we wanted to say. I could sense that he was sad. He was so happy that we were married, but he wanted me to stay longer with him.

On Tuesday, I arrived at the prison in the morning and Andrew held my hand. He took me to the office to get all the things that belonged to him. He was so happy just to be holding my hand, and to be walking that short distance with me; it was maybe 10 metres. We stayed together all day. But there was one other thing that happened on that Tuesday that was amazing.

Andrew's mum, Helen, started to talk to him in Cantonese. She had been doing that for his whole life, and Andrew had only been able to understand the simplest things she said. His brother, Michael, had always translated for them – Andrew spoke English with the rest of the family. But that day, Andrew's mum talked to him in Cantonese about so many things that were important to them both, and Andrew listened. He was also able to speak back to her and to say sorry to her for all the pain he had caused their family. Then we all had lunch together in the prison. While we were eating Andrew said to us, 'Do you know what just happened?' We couldn't guess. Then he said, 'For the first time in my life, I understood every word that my mother said to me. It was a miracle!'

And then at 5 p.m. we had to leave. The seventy-two hours were up and the executions were scheduled for later that evening. There had been another small delay and we were thankful for a few more hours together, but then I had to leave Andrew. We wanted to freeze time. He was a healthy young man. I started to hug him and say goodbye. We were still praying for a miracle. One by one, the other family members also hugged him and said goodbye and they left the visiting room – his brother and then his mum. She was crying and crying. I didn't know what to do. Andrew's lawyer came up to me and said, 'Please, don't cry. If you do, it will break him to pieces.'

So I bit my tongue and I forced myself not to cry. I was the last one to say goodbye. But I didn't say goodbye. I said, 'I love you, Andrew. You know how much I love you. I still hope and I believe.'

He agreed with me. He said, '*Sayang*, I love you too.'

Then, I walked out of the door. There was another room that had our shoes and our bags. I went in there to collect my things and there was a barred window. All the prisoners could walk past the window and see us. I was sitting next to the window and Andrew stood outside and he reached his hands through the bars on the window and he held onto my head and my hand, through that window. I didn't know what to say. I just kissed his hands over and over again. I said, 'I love you.' I didn't say goodbye. I was still hoping that something was going to change.

So I held his hands and I kissed them and I said, 'I love you, Andrew.'

And that was it. It was the last time that I saw him alive.

12

Sing it Louder!

*For God so loved the world that he gave his one
and only Son, that whoever believes in him shall
not perish but have eternal life.*

John 3:16

We were taken to a safe house near the water, where the media couldn't find us. We weren't allowed to be close enough to hear the gunshot. They said that it would traumatise us. But I was so sad. I wanted to be there with Andrew at the end. I had been there for him for all those years, and if you asked me again, I would still say that I wanted to be there with him at the end.

Instead, I sent him my last letter. I wrote, 'Darling, I love you so much. And I still believe in miracles, like the story of Lazarus. God can bring you back to life. But I also want to say . . . when you see Jesus, if you're happy there, please stay. I'd rather you came back. I *want* you to come back. But if you want to stay, stay. Don't worry about me. I wish I could see Jesus together with you, but I know that my time has not come yet. Darling, please keep singing when they take you. Keep singing when you get to the field. Sing! The angels are with you. Jesus is close to you! I'll see you soon. Death cannot separate us. I love you.'

At the same time, Andrew wrote his last letter to me. It was the saddest letter I have ever read. He poured out his feelings. He begged God to give him another chance. He talked about the life he wanted to live with me. He wasn't sure if I would be able to move on. He was so sad and honest. He had already written to me that morning, but he wrote to me again that night. But he also said thank you. He said thank you for everything I had done for him, and even for teaching him how to listen to people and how to be a friend. Then he told me that he wanted me to continue with our vision for the island of Savu; and he told me that he loved me.

At the end, David Soper was allowed to go with him to the field, the place of execution. They had prayed together that morning, and David told me about it later. He said that as they walked across the ground to the spot, the Nigerian in the group started to scream, 'I forgive the president!' and Andrew shouted three times, 'Lord God, please bless Indonesia! Bless Indonesia! Bless Indonesia!' and they all began to sing.

They sang the songs that Andrew had learned and loved and played on his guitar in Kerobokan Prison – 'Amazing Grace', 'Mighty to Save' and '10,000 Reasons'.

Over the years, Andrew had learned those songs and sung them every day in prison (in Kerobokan Prison and then on Nusa Kambangan); even the guards had started to learn the songs and sing them too. They liked those songs. At the end, while the prisoners were walking across the field to the end, they were all singing, 'Mighty to Save' and then 'Amazing Grace' and Andrew said, 'Sing it louder!' They did, they sang it louder. But as they walked over the uneven ground, their voices became softer in that environment, so Andrew said it again, 'Sing it louder!' He said, 'Come on, boys, we can sing better than this!' And they did. They sang it louder and louder. Apparently, the guards began to weep.

Then they arrived at the place of execution. Andrew had been allowed to wear his favourite Penrith Panthers jersey as he walked across the field. When he arrived, he took the jersey off and underneath was a plain white T-shirt with a cross over his heart. The snipers didn't want to miss. Andrew was tied to the pole by his arms and his feet. He had already told the guards that he didn't want a blindfold. He wanted to look those who executed him in the eyes and to pray for them as they fired the guns.

Once each of the prisoners were tied to the poles, they all began to sing '10,000 Reasons' loudly. It was the same song that we had sung on our wedding day.

As the prisoners sang, they managed to finish the first verse and they began the second verse. They were up to the last lines of the second verse, 'Let me be singing / When the evening comes'. Then the shots were fired.

At about 1 a.m., early on Wednesday morning, an embassy official called Andrew's brother, Michael, and he said, 'It's finished. It's over.'

I couldn't believe it. I started to cry. Everyone was weeping. It didn't seem real. I felt like my whole body had gone numb.

The day before, Andrew and I had talked about it. Andrew said that he wanted us to take his body back to Australia. He said that he wanted us to pray him back to life. He really believed that God could raise him from the dead, and if that happened, it would be an incredible, worldwide testimony to the power of God.

So, that's what we did. First of all, Andrew's body was taken to a funeral house in Jakarta and then we took his body on the same plane with us back to Australia. We flew into Sydney on Friday 1 May 2015. It was what Andrew wanted. They put his body in a funeral house in Sydney. The funeral service wasn't until the 8th May, so on Saturday, the 2nd May, we all went to the funeral house. It was a small group of Andrew's close friends and family.

I remember that Michael went inside the room first. He said he wanted to check that everything was all right and that seeing Andrew wouldn't traumatise us. Michael came back out and said that it was OK for us to go in. He ushered me in first. Andrew's body was lying in a white coffin in the corner. I walked over to where he lay and I looked slowly at his face. At first, I didn't recognise him. It didn't look like him. It didn't look like my Andrew. The left side of his face and his body was all bloated and swollen. But then I saw his right side, and I knew that it was him. I couldn't believe it. I felt his hands and his face. He was so cold. I couldn't believe how cold and still he was.

We decided to pray and fast over him. We laid our hands on his cold body. We were all kneeling down, and everyone was being led by God in prayer. We prayed for hours and hours until one lady came up and spoke to Mark Soper, the youngest of David and Shelley's sons and an ordained pastor.

The lady said, 'I've had a word from Jesus . . . and Jesus said that Andrew has chosen to stay there in heaven.'

I was shocked. It was what my last letter to Andrew was about, on the night before he died. I had said that he could stay. But I immediately thought that I should have told him to come back. We were only married for thirty-five hours! It would have been the greatest testimony to God's power if Andrew had come back to life. That was my human thought. I thought it would bring God so much glory. I was so angry. I said to Mark and to the others, 'Tell Jesus that Andrew needs to come back and tell me himself!' Even if he had come back for a little bit . . . I was so angry with Andrew for not coming back. I was so angry at myself for telling him he could stay. And I was so angry at Jesus.

That's when I really started to cry. I cried and I cried. That's when the reality hit me. Andrew chose to stay. He was not coming back. It hit me so very hard.

After that, I saw Andrew's body one more time. He had really gone.

I felt numb all over. I walked out of the funeral house and I didn't know where I was. Andrew was really not coming back. I was crying on the busy road. He was dead. I wasn't going to see him any more, ever again, in this world. I wasn't going to pray with him or talk with him or hug him. I would never feel his arms around me again. I was standing on the main road, crying and crying. I didn't know where I was. I couldn't walk any more. My sister-in-law came and cried with me, and then she walked me to her car.

I thought I was going to go crazy. The darkness was terrible. I couldn't speak with Andrew ever again, after years of speaking to him and praying with him. I felt like I'd lost the greatest treasure I'd ever had in the world – a diamond. I couldn't find it, and I didn't know if I could find anything ever again.

13

He Finished Well

I have fought the good fight. I have finished the race, I have kept the faith.

2 Timothy 4:7

Andrew's funeral was held on Friday, the 8th May, at Baulkham Hills, in Sydney, New South Wales. The family had been searching for a space that was large enough to fit a big crowd, as well as a church that could do live streaming. They knew that there were lots of people who wanted to attend the service but couldn't come, and they wanted to watch it live. Most of the local churches said that they couldn't do live streaming, but the people at Hillsong (a megachurch in Sydney) said, 'Yes, it's easy. We do live streaming every Sunday.' And so it was organised.

The people at Hillsong also said they would help us with everything – the flowers, the booklet and the ushers. It was so amazing. We had all come to the end of our strength. We had nothing left, and they really helped us. We were under so much pressure, and we were grateful for them.

Fifteen hundred people came to the service. As we walked in, they handed us the order of service with a picture of Andrew on the cover and the words beneath it from 2 Timothy 4:7: 'I have fought the good fight, I have finished the race, I have kept the faith.'

Mark Soper led the service. He welcomed everyone. He introduced the worship team, which included the Riddington family. They knew Andrew well and they loved him. They had visited him in Kerobokan Prison from the beginning. They had been there since his first trial. They had been on the first flight whenever something happened. They had helped Andrew with his online Bible course. So they shared funny stories about Andrew, throughout the service. They talked about how they had seen such big changes in his life as he came to know Jesus. And we all sang Andrew's favourite songs. I cried and cried, especially when we sang, 'Blessed Be Your Name.' In the last lines the song acknowledges, as Job did in Job 1:21, that the Lord gives and takes away.

Blessed Be Your Name
In the land that is plentiful
Where Your streams of abundance flow
Blessed be Your name

Blessed be Your name
When I'm found in the desert place
Though I walk through the wilderness
Blessed be Your name

Every blessing You pour out
I'll turn back to praise
When the darkness closes in,
Lord still I will say

Blessed be the name of the Lord
Blessed be Your name
Blessed be the name of the Lord
Blessed be Your glorious name

Blessed be Your name
When the sun's shining down on me
When the world's all as it should be
Blessed be Your name

Blessed be Your name
On the road marked with suffering
Though there's pain in the offering
Blessed be Your name

You give and take away
You give and take away
My heart will choose to say
Lord blessed be Your name

Every blessing You pour out
I'll turn back to praise
When the darkness closes in, Lord,
Still I will say

Blessed be the name of the Lord
Blessed be Your name
Blessed be the name of the Lord
Blessed be Your glorious name, oh

Blessed be Your name[3]

We will bless his glorious name, because he's still the Lord. Even when God allows intense pain and suffering and darkness, even when we grieve and go through the hardest times, still we praise him – because he's still the Lord.

A lot of people were crying that day, even those leading worship. In-between the singing, Andrew's brother, Michael, stood up to share. He thanked everyone for coming and spoke about Andrew's transformation. He knew how much Andrew had changed, and he said that he was amazed by the impact of Andrew's changed life. He had seen it. Then Michael said, 'People deserve a second chance in life. People make mistakes in life and they deserve a second chance. Andrew showed me that everyone can change, and change for the better.'

Then it was my turn to get up and share about Andrew. I stood there and I looked out at the crowd that had gathered. It was only eleven days since our wedding ceremony on Nusa Kambangan. I looked at them and I admitted that I had done more preparations for his funeral service than I had done for our own wedding service. Then I said that I also had so many good stories that I could share about Andrew. I loved him. I had seen how much he had loved Jesus. Then I read out the last letters that we had sent to each other on the night before he was executed.

I admitted as well, though, that I had many questions in my heart and my mind. Millions of people had prayed for Andrew. Why did God not answer us? Why did we not see a miracle? Why did the president not change his mind? It seemed to us as if nothing happened. What about the shared vision we had for the island of Savu? Andrew and I had prayed together every single day, but it seemed like our prayers for a miracle had not been answered.

But then I said that I also had to face what had happened. I had to keep trusting Jesus. And I said that Andrew ended well. I felt that no one could ever face death like him. Even as Andrew walked to the field, he was very calm. He prayed that God would forgive the ones holding the rifles. He prayed for the guards. He said, 'Lord, please bless Indonesia!' and he sang praise songs to God, right till the end. He finished so well. Where did he get the courage? How can someone face death and be so strong? How did Andrew do that? The answer is that he trusted Jesus. Andrew managed to end it well and bless people and forgive those who hurt him – and it was only because of Jesus. If any of us (wherever we are – in prison or on the outside) want to have the same courage and peace in our lives, then we will only find it through Jesus.

'Yes,' I said to them, 'it's so very hard to understand, but I believe that God has a better plan for us . . .'

Then the service was over. Mark spoke again to that huge crowd. He prayed for all of us and invited us to trust Jesus. He said, 'If you have received Jesus for the first time today, or if you would like to receive Jesus, then please pray now (on your own or with someone) and please take a Bible on your way out.' The ushers had been given Bibles to hand out to anyone who didn't own one and who asked for one. Later, they told us that more than two hundred people took a Bible on their way out that day. We were all amazed.

In the days following the funeral, letters and emails came from hundreds of people who had watched the service all around the world. Some testified to the fact that they had recommitted their lives to Christ, and others shared that the story and testimony of Andrew's life had led them to faith in Jesus.

Afterwards, they gave us Andrew's ashes. We buried them eight months later, on his birthday, in Rookwood Cemetery, Sydney.

14

Darkness

But I cry to you for help, LORD; in the morning my prayer comes before you. Why, LORD, do you reject me and hide your face from me?

Psalm 88:13,14

The funeral was over. It had gone well; it was what Andrew wanted. He finished well. But my journey of grief was only just beginning. One night some months later, I woke up in the middle of the night, and I stood up and grabbed my jacket. It was 2 a.m. and I had an overwhelming feeling that I needed to go and find Andrew. I believed I could find him, even if I had to search to the ends of the earth. It was so real. I had to find him! I knew that I could find him! I opened the door of my room and my brain slowly started to say, 'No, Feby, he's dead.'

I went back inside and sat down on my bed. I felt so angry and confused and despairing. I knew that I needed help. I didn't understand. What was God doing? Was I losing my mind? Why did God send me so clearly to Andrew, for this to happen? I believed that a miracle could occur. I knew it could. That's why it was so shocking. I had so much confidence that God would do a miracle. God sent me to Andrew with so much confirmation. I never thought that he would die.

Up until then, I hadn't wanted to go for counselling. I kept refusing to talk to anyone. I kept to myself. I didn't feel that I could trust anyone. I knew that it would leak out to the media, even if I just told my family and friends.

Throughout it all, the media had been chasing us, and they only ever picked up on one angle, without the context of the whole story. It seemed to me that they made up their own story in order to sell it, to make money and stay in business. Whenever I was in Bali, coming and going from Kerobokan Prison, they were always after me, always shoving the camera in my face, especially after the final appeal for clemency was rejected back in January.

I was thankful for some friends who tried to protect me, but whenever I turned on the television or the radio back then, Andrew's story would be on the news, his face staring at me from the screen at least every second night. It was heart-wrenching. So I turned the television off. I learned not to read anything or listen to anything. I tried to avoid it. But the media didn't go away. Even when we were on Nusa Kambangan Island at the end, they used telephoto lenses from another island. Even a photo taken at our wedding was somehow leaked to the media. Someone made money from it, and the public saw it before I did. It was one of only five photos that were taken of that day. It upset me so much. Even when we arrived at Sydney Airport with Andrew's body, they were waiting for us behind the fence with their zoom lenses. It added to the trauma and the ongoing need to hide and keep to myself.

Every night that year, I had another execution dream. I would be walking to the execution field and I would be crying and saying, 'I want to go with you!' and every night, in my dreams, Andrew would say nothing in reply. He would just be silent.

Then each morning I would wake up with pain in my whole body: there was pain in my chest; I would be aching. And every morning I woke up crying. I wanted to run away from everything. I didn't want to feel the pain, but everywhere I went, the pain came with me.

Then that night when I went looking for Andrew in the middle of the night, I knew that I had almost lost my mind. So I emailed my friend Eugen. He and his wife were in Iraq at the time, ministering to women and children who had run away from ISIS. I told Eugen that I needed to get away. I said, 'Can I come and visit you both in Iraq?' I thought to myself that maybe if I got hit by a bomb in Iraq then that would be good. I knew that I couldn't kill myself, but if I went to Iraq and had an accident, then it wouldn't be my fault.

Eugen emailed me back and he also contacted my friends. He knew that I needed help. He suggested I visit an organisation that was involved in inner healing. I went four times for counselling. It allowed me to see how messed up my mind was. It helped me to put things back in the right place. My mind was so messy.

After those sessions, I knew that I needed more than talking. I needed worship. When Andrew died, and after we saw his body in the funeral house, I had stopped praying and singing. I was so angry with God.

I had to start again. In December 2015, I went to South Africa to see a friend. I was desperate. I wanted to get away from both Indonesia and Australia. I had to get away from the reminders. My mind didn't know what to do. Being in a new environment was good, but I missed talking to Andrew, and I missed talking to people who knew Andrew. I woke up one morning, closed my eyes and said, 'God, I don't know what to do.'

In that moment, something rose up in my chest. It burst out. The words came out: 'Who am I to question you?' Some part of my spirit understood that something wasn't right inside me. I had stopped praying and worshipping God for eight months (after being someone who worshipped God every day, for six hours a day) and I suddenly knew – who was I to question God's plans?

I started to cry and cry. I began to talk to God. I said that I didn't understand why it had happened. It was so hard and painful. What exactly did he want from me?

That's how I slowly started to talk to God again. And at the same time as talking to God, I started to read the Bible once more, in January 2016. I began with the Psalms and the stories that I knew would comfort me. I didn't read anything that I knew would be hard. So I read about Mary, the mother of Jesus. I read the first two chapters of Luke's Gospel over and over again. It was so hard for Mary to be found pregnant in that society. She must have felt the shame and disgrace. Back then, in that society, she could have been stoned to death, and yet they called it 'favour'. When the angel came to speak with Mary, he said to her, 'Do not be afraid, Mary, you have found favour with God' (Luke 1:30).

I had no idea, until then, that people could be entrusted with difficult times – for 'such a time as this' (Esth. 4:14) – and that it could be called 'favour'. I had always thought that God entrusts us with good gifts or with good things and opportunities. Favour should lead to good things! But during that time, I slowly began to realise that God also entrusts us with very difficult things, like when Mary carried Jesus. It was so hard for her. Even after Jesus was born, they had to travel from one place to another to avoid being killed. Yet the angel called it 'favour'. Maybe Mary also thought about that, and maybe she held on to the idea of favour. What does it mean for us to find favour with God? I think that if I had been Mary, I would have thought something good and big was going to happen! Yet, instead, Mary felt the shame of falling pregnant before she was married, and then she saw her son executed on a cross in front of her eyes. This was called 'favour'.

At the same time, I read about the disciple Peter. He must have felt terrible grief after Jesus died. We know that Peter immediately went back to his old habits, fishing on the Sea of Galilee (John 21). Jesus had called Peter to be a fisher of people (Matt. 4:18–20), but as soon as Jesus died, Peter went back to his old habits. That's where Jesus found him again, as he stood on the shoreline, in John 21. I thought, 'If even Peter can be like that (so lost in his grief after losing Jesus), then maybe my journey of grief is also understandable. Maybe it makes sense.' Peter had been travelling with Jesus: he had heard everything that Jesus said, he had seen everything that Jesus did, and yet he was filled with grief and disappointment. Also, he must have felt like a failure. Peter denied Jesus three times at the house of Caiaphas (Matt. 26:69–75) while Jesus was under arrest and trial. Peter failed Jesus. It showed me about the human condition. We are all like that. I am like that.

I realised as I read the Gospels again, and thought about Peter, that I had seen so many miracles in my life, and yet I had stopped praying and believing. I had stopped worshipping God. I had spent my whole life praying, and even been employed to pray, and yet I had stopped talking to God, and I had stopped trusting in him. Before that, I might have said that one big encounter with God, once in your life or even once a year, is really important. I would have said that's what we need! But I started to see, after Andrew died, that we need an encounter with Jesus every single day, not just once in our lives or once a year. We need to come to God daily, even when we feel as though we can't.

So I started to pray again, but it was hard. In 2016, every month there was a new anniversary – our birthdays in January and February, and the day we got engaged in Kerobokan Prison, and the day we got married on Nusa Kambangan Island, and the execution. As I said earlier, I had pain in my body – chest pain. I couldn't watch the news. If I saw an accident, or watched a movie that involved killing, I would suddenly become angry and I couldn't breathe. It was actual chest pain. It went on for a long time. I tried to pray. I thought about going back to the ministry or starting to share my story with others. I even tried to share a few times at different churches who invited me, but it wasn't right. I realised that my sharing was coming from a place of anger, not from the right place. I wasn't ready yet. I realised that people who are grieving need to wait until they're ready. Sometimes we try to do things too soon.

At about that time, I read the story of Thomas (John 20:24–29). Thomas wanted to see Jesus for himself. All of the disciples had heard the promises. They had heard Jesus say that he would be raised from the dead (Matt. 16:21), but after Jesus died, the fear came down, and all the disciples locked themselves in the upper room, terrified (John 20:19). Even after they encountered the risen Christ, they were still afraid (John 20:26). As I read that part of the Gospels, I slowly started to understand why they did it. I understood Thomas's doubts for the first time. Then, as I read on, I began to see what happened next, in Acts chapters 1 and 2. From the downfall and betrayal and grief and awful pain came the harvest: thousands of people coming to know the Lord Jesus, in Acts 2, and then more and more after that. I slowly began to feel the tiniest bit of hope.

For most of 2016, I also tried to stay around godly, positive people who had a strong faith in the Lord Jesus and who were close to Andrew and me. I did that deliberately. I also didn't read the newspapers. I avoided negative people and those who knew nothing about Andrew. I realised how important it was to guard my heart, as it says in Proverbs 4:23: 'Above all else, guard your heart, for everything you do flows from it.' I slowly built up my prayer time. I just stayed in the presence of God whenever I could – and now I know what's so important with grieving people. Just be there for them. Don't try to say something. Don't say anything at all, actually, especially when you know nothing about their situation.

Some people said to me, 'At least you only knew Andrew for a short time. Imagine how hard it would have been if you had known him for a long time.'

I felt like saying to them, 'I wanted to know him forever!'

Other people said to me, 'Well, at least he's in a better place.'

I felt like saying to them, 'Well, that's good for him, but here I am on earth, living with this terrible memory for the rest of my life.'

Still other people told me how much his life and testimony had been used by God, for good purposes. They said, 'Be thankful. Andrew brought a lot of people to Jesus!'

I felt like saying to them, 'Well, that's good for them, but what about me? I'm here in pain.'

They all tried to comfort me. They were doing their best, and I was so grateful for their care, but they didn't understand. What I needed was for people to grieve with me, sit with me and be quiet; not to try to fix me or even comfort me – just to be there. They didn't have to say anything at all. There are no words that are good enough to really comfort. Any words (even the nicest words) at that time will hurt because every good word can be twisted to sound like the wrong word when someone is in pain.

Back then, I don't think I realised that God had actually answered my prayer the night before Andrew had died. I had told Andrew in my final letter that he could stay in heaven if he wanted to, and then God had sent the lady in the funeral house who told me, via Mark, exactly what had happened. Andrew had chosen to stay with Jesus, and I had said to him, 'If you want to stay, stay' – but I didn't listen. I was so angry with God, and with Andrew, because he had chosen to stay! It didn't really cross my mind until afterwards that heaven is so beautiful. Of course Andrew wanted to stay. I would have wanted to go to be with Jesus too – but it was so hard staying on earth without him. I just really wanted to see Andrew again. The biggest grief was that I couldn't talk to him or see his face or hear his voice or hold him. The feeling of separation was intense. It still is. It's not about whether he is in heaven or hell. I know where he is!

My favourite reminder was in Romans 12:15: 'Rejoice with those who rejoice; mourn with those who mourn.' That's what we need to do – we need to sit and mourn with those who mourn. When people grieved with me, I felt strengthened. I knew they understood me. The Sopers did that really well for me, and so did the three other families – the Wilkinses, the Riddingtons and the Bairds. They just said, 'Sit down, Feby,' and, 'Do you want coffee?' They didn't say anything else. They were just there for me. They showed up in my life and I knew that I wasn't alone.

15

Until That Day

*He makes me lie down in green pastures, he leads
me beside quiet waters, he refreshes my soul.*
                                        Psalm 23:2,3

I have learned, slowly, that God has a perfect will, and it's not
the same as my own will. I have to trust him, in everything. He
is still God, and he is still good, even in the hardest of times or
even if the outcome is not the one that I am expecting. I have
to trust that he is still faithful and good, even when my prayers
aren't answered in the way that I want.

I have also learned that God says to us, 'Don't be afraid to go
through the darkest times, if you have Jesus with you. He will
comfort you. He will be with you.' But I don't think that we are
meant to stay in the darkest times. There is a crushing of the
soul, and depression, but we are not meant to stay there. There
are reasons why we have to go through that, but it's not forever.

Over the next two years I had my ups and downs. There
was a lot of crying and anger. In 2016 I spent time in prayer
with two of my friends, including Linda. They both had experience in counselling people with inner healing, so they took
me gently through that process – praying for the feelings of
being abandoned and rejected, dealing with the root cause of

the problem. It brought out more of my grief, even associated with losing my dad when I was 15. I hadn't expected that. My dad died exactly twenty years before Andrew died. I had been close to my dad, so the grief of losing Andrew made the loss of my dad feel more intense. I hadn't been able to be with my dad when he died, in Surabaya, Java, and I hadn't been able to be with Andrew, on that field, when the shots were fired.

The hardest part was that I questioned God and his love for me. Does he really love me? What if he doesn't? How could he hurt me like this? How could he take away someone whom I really loved? If he had the power to stop it, why didn't he?

My friends kept praying with me and they helped me to slowly deal with my grief over my dad, and the terrible loss of Andrew. They helped me to get to the point of letting go of all the things that I couldn't understand. There were so many things! There still are.

I slowly started to feel a little bit better. I began to spend more time in worship, bit by bit, listening to God. I built up gradually. In the beginning, I worried that if I read the Bible, I might question it. I knew that I wanted to trust God again, but I was worried that I might not be able to. So, as I mentioned earlier, I read the verses and stories that I knew would comfort me, like the ones about Mary and Peter and Thomas, and I read Psalm 23 over and over again.

Then finally, in 2017, I decided that I could go back to Savu and continue with the plans that we had for the community centre and for the island. I felt a bit better. By then, I had not visited Savu since 2014, but the plans we had made back then were still in progress. We had decided on the building proposal. My uncle had given us a block of land, but we hadn't done anything with it yet, apart from making the plans.

So I began to think that it was time for me to go back to Savu and start work on the community centre for the children. But I was a little bit reluctant. Why would I help a nation like Indonesia that had decided not to help Andrew?

In early 2017, I spent three days fasting and praying, in Yogyakarta. I went back up to the prayer house on Mount Merapi (where I had prayed with Linda in January 2012) and I stayed there for three days. I prayed to God and I said, 'I want to hear from you one more time about Savu and the community centre.'

On the third and final day, God spoke to me very clearly, even more clearly than before. He said, 'It's not about you, Feby, or even about Andrew. It's about my kingdom and my people on that island.' He said, 'Stop looking at yourself and your own pain. It's about my kingdom.'

At the time, it felt like a bit of a slap in the face, although a kind one, and I knew I needed it. God slowly and gently showed me how self-centred I had become. I felt a bit ashamed and embarrassed. I had been looking at myself and my own pain, rather than at God. But ultimately, it helped. It made me stronger.

So I said to God, 'OK, Lord, if this is what you want, if this is for your kingdom, then I will do it.'

I went back to Savu in March 2017, and I started to build. Some friends helped me with the plans and design for the centre. Then I found the workers. I had to learn from YouTube how to build the centre. Of course, I wasn't doing the hands-on work myself, but I needed to understand it, if the workers asked me a question – and they asked me lots of questions! The workers would say things such as, 'How much sand and cement do you want us to use in the mix?' and, 'What size rocks do you want us to use in the walls?' I had no idea what they were talking about, so I googled it and called my family (although connection was difficult) and we tried to work it out together. One of my sisters was by then working as a civil engineer in Papua, so she helped a lot. When I couldn't get a connection, I climbed up a tree and googled it.

I kept visiting Savu, on and off, for most of 2017. The building supervisor had told me how much the community centre would cost and how long it would take to build, but it took twice as long as he said. There was always 'not enough of this' or 'not enough of that'. We had to regularly get supplies from another island.

Then the workers asked for the rest of the money, even though they hadn't finished the building. I said no. I knew that it wasn't right. The next day, the supervisor came to the centre with fifteen young men. It was late afternoon – and he asked me for the money. He threatened me.

I said, 'I am a woman, here by myself, and you have brought all these men with you. What are you trying to do?' I knew it was disrespectful. So I called the head of the village to come to help me. He came, and we all sat down on the sand in front of the centre, and we talked very calmly, but firmly.

I said to the workers, 'I have the money here, but you are not getting it until you finish the building.' The head of the village supported me.

The next day, the supervisor sent people to finish the work, and they did as they were told. In the meantime, though, my family were worried about me. I had told them that the community centre was for ministry. 'Stay calm,' I said. 'It could have gone very badly, but it didn't.'

After the centre itself was finished, we built a playground with climbing frames, seesaws and swings in front of the centre.

There was nothing else like it on the whole island of Savu. We went to the mountains nearby and found some big trees to use to build it. It was my job to choose the trees and the workers used the chainsaws to cut them down. Together, we brought them back to the centre and we built the playground.

Then we dug the well! During the building of the centre, we had been using another well, from another place nearby. I was so excited to dig our own well. It was what Andrew had always wanted and what he had often asked me about. He knew that Savu was a dry island and that water was a real problem there, so he would often say to me, '*Sayang*, don't forget about the well! We need to dig the well so that the children can have water.' So as soon as we finished the well, all I could think about was how happy Andrew would have been. He would have been jumping around, saying, 'We did it, *Sayang*! We built the well!'

That's where I am now, as I write this, five years since Andrew's death – at our new community centre on the island of Savu. We have 120 children at the centre when they all come. Sometimes it's only thirty or sixty. Every day, we provide English, music, reading, writing, painting and sport. The children love to read. When I opened the library, they were so excited about the books, which were all bilingual. The children's English has really improved!

When we started, my emphasis was on a good education. I knew that I needed to provide good resources for the children to improve their literacy. I thought that if we wanted to see changes in Indonesia, then we would have to begin with education and literacy. But what kind of education do we actually want the children to have? What kind of values? For a while, I was so immersed in thinking about their education that I forgot about spending time in teaching them about God.

When I started to talk to the teenagers, I realised that it was very hard to change their mindset. They were already so exposed to the society and the values around them. So that was when we focused more on the younger children, giving them godly values. If we wanted to change the nation, we realised that we needed to impact the youngest generation first. Then, we thought, in ten years' time those children will change the whole island. If they go into the government system with those values, they will change the system and then the nation.

In my case, it started with the children themselves. One day, a group of the children asked me if they could have a Bible study. I was so happy when they asked me that! We decided to run it on Saturdays.

When we began, I started by reading Psalm 23. I love Psalm 23, and the children understand it. All of the children on the island have animals – pigs, goats and chickens. They depend on their animals for survival, and they love them. So whenever they read Psalm 23, they understand it. They know that they have to look after their animals! One little boy told me that he ran back home every day at 3 p.m. to feed his pigs.

I said to him, 'Even you understand this psalm – and actually the Lord is the same as you are (in that way). The Lord is a really good shepherd! He's the best shepherd. He loves us. Psalm 23 says, "The LORD is my shepherd, I lack nothing. He makes me lie down in green pastures, he leads me beside quiet waters, he refreshes my soul." The Lord is like that! He knows when we need feeding or when we get sick. He always cares for us, no matter what.'

Now, most days at the centre we have Bible devotions, and the children write down verses in their little copy books that I give them. At the moment, we're in the Gospel of Mark. They just read one verse every day. They write it at the top of the page, and then, at the bottom of the page, they write down their prayer list.

I say to them, 'You don't have to show anyone your prayer list. That's personal. It's just between you and God.' But they usually show me their prayer lists. Then I also write in their books. Sometimes I write down prayer requests that they can pray for me. Recently, I asked the children to pray for teachers to come to the island. It's so hard to find teachers! Then, after a lot of prayer, a teacher actually came to the island last year, a qualified teacher. She was exactly what we needed, and the kids said, 'God answers prayer!' We could give thanks as well as pray!

Every Saturday, now, about ten children come to the Bible study. After Psalm 23, we started to read Psalm 91 – just one verse every week. After a few weeks, we came to verse 5. It says, 'You will not fear the terror of night, nor the arrow that flies by day . . .'

I said to the children, 'Go home and think about what that verse means – the terror of the night. Why is it scary at night? How does God help us when we're scared and afraid?'

That same night, I walked home after school with five of the children. It was so dark. There was no electricity in the area. Then suddenly we saw a mango tree and a coconut tree on fire! We went to the place where the fire was, and there was a house in-between the two trees. Part of the house was also on fire. So I told the children to go and get some water. But it was the dry season; the children came back and told me there was no water. What could we do? I said, 'Get some sand!' but it was too late. The roof was made of palm leaves and it was already burning down and spreading to the main house.

I said to the children, 'We must pray!'

They said, 'Should we pray for rain?'

I felt I didn't have enough faith at that moment to pray for rain. It never rains in the dry season. So I said, 'Just ask God to stop the fire.'

The children prayed and prayed, and the fire stopped, just like that. We walked home. And the children said, 'Wow, the Bible is true! It was just like Psalm 91.'

That kind of thing has been happening very often here. The Bible is becoming real to the children and I know that they will remember it for the rest of their lives. They know that the God that they worship is not very far away. They are each starting to have visions of Jesus, and they understand who they are in Christ; they know that they are loved and shown grace, through the death and resurrection of Jesus. They know that in trusting Jesus, they have become part of God's family. I will keep praying for revival in this village. The children believe in prayer, and the prayer lists in their books are becoming longer and longer.

Nowadays, the children also teach me about prayer, and about how to trust God. Even here on Savu, it took me a long time to build up my trust in God and my faith. That was the hardest part. Would he not hurt me again? Was it worth it – to go through all that pain? Could I trust God again?

For a long time, I felt betrayed. If God was a human friend, I would find it hard to trust him again. But then I slowly realised that God never told me that he was going to keep Andrew alive. I just assumed that, or I expected a miracle.

I said to Linda one day, 'Can you please ask God why he did this to me? Why?'

Everyone else said that they didn't understand why, but Linda said to me, 'Perhaps God said you were only meant to be with Andrew until the end. You were meant to be company until that day. Perhaps you were meant to be there to love him, and to build up his faith in Jesus, and to walk him home.'

I think Linda is right. Slowly, God has been showing me that my calling was to accompany Andrew to the very last moment, to walk him home. That was my calling in that situation. God prepared me for it for years. The purpose was about Andrew, and about God's glory; it was about me being the person who could encourage Andrew and love him and support him to the last moments. That's how much God loved Andrew. He gave me to him, to walk him home. I think that God has a way of loving each person differently. He knows what we each need at different times. He's a loving Father.

So I can now call it a privilege and favour, because God really loved Andrew. He chose me to be with him, to comfort him and love him and strengthen him in his faith until the end. Of course, there are scars left behind, and there is always an ache. The scars will stay there, but the wound is slowly healing.

In 2 Corinthians, the apostle Paul said that he was struggling. He said he was weak; he had lots of scars, and even a thorn in his flesh (2 Cor. 12:7). Paul said, 'Three times I pleaded with the Lord to take it away from me. But he said to me, "My grace is sufficient for you, for my power is made perfect in weakness"' (2 Cor. 12:8,9). Paul even thanked God for his weakness and sufferings, because he knew that when he was weak, he was actually strong, in the strength of the Lord. That helps me whenever I read it. For Paul, and for all of us, it is a proof of life to have scars and burdens, but it can also be a testimony to Jesus and the goodness of God in our lives. The scars show that God has brought healing through the cross of Jesus, and the scars show that the strength we have is not from ourselves, but from God.

Now, I've come to see that everyone has scars in their lives, but the scars can be a testimony to bring glory to God. We can't forget. It's impossible. But we have to forgive and let go. And we have to believe that there is power in the resurrection for broken souls.

Every now and again, these days, I hear about the work that continues in Kerobokan Prison. Apparently, after Andrew died, the ministry seemed quieter for a while. There were no new baptisms for four years. Everybody was grieving over Andrew. But God was still at work in that place, in good ways. In 2018, apparently some more money was raised, and they built a new chapel to replace the old one because it had become too small. There is room for all of the people to fit in the new chapel, and there is room for prayer, in the way that Andrew always wanted. In late 2019, there were apparently twenty-six people all asking to be baptised in the pool outside the new chapel. God is still at work, in his marvellous ways and in his perfect timing. He is still mighty to save. And the people are still singing.

As for me, on Savu, I'm praying and singing and worshipping with the children. I know that this is where I'm meant to be, for now. Before I came back to the island, I asked God whether or not I should go back to prison ministry, and the answer was clearly no. God said that my part there was finished. It was so clear. I had done what I was asked to do. But my part on Savu is still ongoing.

I sometimes wonder what Andrew would say to me now, here on Savu. I know that he would say something funny. He would make me laugh! He would also calm me down. He would say, '*Sayang*, relax!' He would say it in his funny way. I can't even describe to you the way he used to say it, but every time, it would make me laugh. Even now, I sometimes say

'Relax!' to my mum, using his Australian accent, and we both laugh because we know that we are remembering him.

I think Andrew would also say to me, 'We did it! We started a community centre, here on Savu, for 120 children!' He would say, 'This is amazing. God is amazing! Jesus is amazing!' Andrew would always use the word 'amazing'.

Of course, he would be right. It *is* amazing. Maybe there are more amazing things yet to come. There are more things that God will do – here on earth and, of course, in heaven.

Glossary

Duku – tropical fruit grown in Java
Nasi kucing – Indonesian snack
Nyai Roro Kidul – the Queen of the Southern Sea
Orang Kuat – strong man
Pad thai – a stir-fried noodle dish
Sayang – honey, darling
Siri pinang – betel nut
Wedang ronde jahe – hot ginger tea

Notes

1 'Mighty To Save', words and music by Ben Fielding & Reuben Morgan © 2006 Hillsong Music Publishing.

2 '10,000 Reasons (Bless The Lord)' written by Matt Redman and Jonas Myrin. Copyright © 2011 Thankyou Music (PRS) (adm. worldwide at CapitolCMGPublishing.com excluding Europe which is adm. by Integrity Music, part of the David C Cook family. Songs@integritymusic.com) / Atlas Mountain Songs (BMI) worshiptogether.com Songs (ASCAP) sixsteps Music (ASCAP) (adm. at CapitolCMGPublishing.com) All rights reserved. Used by permission.

3 'Blessed Be Your Name' written by Beth Redman and Matt Redman. Copyright © 2002 Thankyou Music (PRS) (adm. worldwide at CapitolCMGPublishing.com excluding Europe which is adm. by Integrity Music, part of the David C Cook family. Songs@integritymusic.com) All rights reserved. Used by permission.